Pete Killingley

A CHRISTIAN'S GUIDE TO AI

12 Biblical Answers to the Questions We're All Asking

thegoodbook COMPANY

A Christian's Guide to AI

Published by:
The Good Book Company

thegoodbook.com | thegoodbook.co.uk
thegoodbook.com.au | thegoodbook.co.nz

All emphasis in Scripture quotations have been added by the author.

Titles published by The Good Book Company may be purchased in bulk for educational, business, fundraising or sales promotional use. For information and bespoke pricing, please email SpecialMarkets@thegoodbook.com.

Every book published by The Good Book Company has been written by a human author and edited by a human editor. While AI tools are sometimes used to assist with research and support certain processes, all content has been created by a human author and thoroughly checked by our editorial team to ensure it is biblically faithful and pastorally wise.

Cover design by Drew McCall

ISBN: 9781802544268 | JOB-008838 | Printed in India

"I confess to having been a bit 'head-in-the-sand' about AI—avoiding it seems easier than learning how to engage in an informed and godly way. I'm so thankful to Pete for producing this accessible and immensely helpful book. He addresses the questions we all need to grapple with, applying the timeless wisdom of God's word to each with grace, humility and an appropriate amount of humour! An invaluable resource."

CAROLYN LACEY, Author, *Amazed*

"As AI use accelerates, some of our oldest questions get sharper. What does it really mean to be human? To work, to create, to relate, and to bear responsibility? Pete Killingley addresses these questions and more with Bible in hand, helping us engage with new technologies without losing our hold on God's truth. This is a wise biblical guide for navigating complex technological terrain while following and trusting the God who remains Lord over it all."

MATT LILLICRAP, CEO, UCCF

"Pete has written a very helpful primer for Christians on engaging with AI. It is well researched, makes helpful distinctions and offers wise advice. He asks really excellent discussion questions which press the reader to decide what they will do in various arenas. This will make you a better user of AI."

MATT FULLER, Author, *Reclaiming Masculinity*

"As the church begins to grapple with the implications of AI, we need resources that are theologically and pastorally wise. Pete Killingley offers exactly that. This book provides a clear and thoughtful introduction to vital questions that followers of Jesus should be asking about AI. This is a timely and valuable resource that will help equip the church to respond with wisdom, clarity and faithfulness in a rapidly changing world."

DAVID BETTS, Author, *The Church and AI*

"There is every indication that AI may prove to be one of the most powerful and important technologies of our time. We cannot sit idly by but must instead learn what AI is, what benefits it may bring to our lives, and what drawbacks it may exact from them. I'm thankful that Pete Killingley models that kind of deliberate examination and careful engagement in *A Christian's Guide to AI*."

TIM CHALLIES, Author, *The Next Story*

"Pete Killingley has done a great service to the church. With wit and wisdom, he guides us through the strange, new world of AI, avoiding both hand-wringing doom and gushing about the utopia on offer. Instead, from solid research and biblical application, he shows us both the possibilities and temptations that AI presents. The book is really about how to preserve human dignity and integrity when faced with a new technology. If you care about being truly human in today's AI-infused world, read this book."

TED TURNAU, Author, *Popologetics*

"With clarity and accessibility, Pete gently draws the reader through the questions he raises about AI and our relationship with it. I love that this book is rooted in Scripture and shaped by the lived experience of an author who is a father, pastor and someone helping the church engage in the public square. He models how to ask the right critical questions about AI, holding them alongside the hope we have in Christ. This is a thoughtful and grounded guide."

ROSS HENDRY, CEO, CARE

"If only we had a helpful, biblical, thoughtful 'primer' to get us thinking straight and establish some wise boundaries around AI. We do! And this is it. Pete's book is clear, measured and rooted in Scripture. It steers a useful course between extremes and shows how Christians can think soberly about the world God has placed us in. I benefitted greatly from reading this from cover to cover (without an AI summary), and you will too."

ADRIAN REYNOLDS, Associate National Director, FIEC

To Sophie.
Thank you for your encouragement—I would never have written this book without it.
Thank you for your joy—life would be so much more boring without you. You are truly superfluous.

Will the robotic leader come at last to achieve our objective,
feed the hungry, forgive the debtors, heal the sick,
give sight to the blind, release the captives, raise the dead?

...

Or do we look for another?

—Wendell Berry, Sabbaths 2014

Contents

Introduction

One thing I learned when I started this project is that if you tell people that you're writing a book on AI, around 50% of the responses you'll get are jokes about getting AI to write it for you.

ChatGPT did not write this book. I have, however, made use of AI at many points in the process. I'll tell you how I've used it, both because I think transparency is important and to show you some of the positives about AI right from the beginning. Because many of the chapters that follow are cautious, encouraging us as Christians to think carefully about how we use AI and why, it might come across as if I'm against it. But AI can be a fantastic tool if used rightly and wisely.

Here are the ways it came in handy (or not) during the book-writing process. I've used AI...

- to give me book recommendations for helpful background reading.

- as a search engine—to help me find reliable sources for statistics I've come across, rediscover news articles I recall seeing previously, or find quotes which I half remember. AI is much easier than Google if you don't remember the exact words.

- to list Bible verses on a certain theme (for example, all Bible verses on friendship from the book of Proverbs). I can't prove that it was exhaustive, but for each verse it gave, I then looked it up for myself, so I know it didn't give me any false positives.
- to translate a report on AI from German into English.
- to summarise research papers so that I can know whether I'm likely to gain relevant information by reading the whole paper.
- to transcribe voice notes. Often, when I'm walking, my thoughts crystallise, and I record a voice note. Rather than listen back to each note back and type them all up, I get AI to transcribe them for me, saving me time.
- as a case study. I've probed and prodded AI to see what kinds of answers it gives me. Although it makes this mistake less frequently than it used to, I was delighted when I asked it how many times the letter "r" appears in strawberry and it got it wrong (see chapter 3).
- to help produce endnotes.
- as dictation software. I ditched this pretty quickly because I'm a fast typist and it actually slowed me down.
- for an initial edit or review. I've uploaded sections and asked it to point out where my argument is weak or needs refining. I've asked it to show me where I've typed extraneous words or incomplete sentences.

- for the chapter on whether AI can ever be like us. I'd written an illustration which referred to the droids in Star Wars (C3PO and R2D2). The theological point I was making was accurate, but I'm not so familiar with the films that I could know if the illustration was truly helpful. I asked AI to take on the persona of a pedantic Star Wars fan and then critique what I'd written. On the basis of its feedback (and input from my wife and daughter), I deleted that paragraph.

I use AI confidently yet cautiously. In the areas where I believe it's ethical to use it, I give clear instructions and then test everything. I never blindly trust information given to me by AI and always double-check primary sources. Where mistakes remain, I take full responsibility. It's my fault, not AI's!

Why This Book?

A common view of the church is that we're always a few years behind the world when it comes to any cultural or technological change. Whether that's true or not, we should be asking where we *want* to be as churches: at the forefront of the change or picking up the pieces of the people AI leaves in its wake?

As Christians, we do need to start thinking about AI deliberately. The fact that you've picked up this book means you probably agree. It would be so easy for us to split into our camps of tech-lovers and technophobes (you might have guessed I'm in the former category) and then use or not use AI as we each see fit. Because the Bible doesn't give us a handbook for how to relate to AI, we would each create our own guidelines, often without a huge amount of thought.

But as I've studied AI over the last few years and given seminars on the topic to churches and church leaders,

I've been struck that although the Bible doesn't explicitly mention AI, it does give us an abundance of theological themes that help us understand the AI revolution. Whether that be our theology of humanity, of technology, of creativity, of work, of friendship or of the future, the Bible is not silent.

And so we're going to explore twelve questions that Christians ask about AI. My hope and prayer is that it helps us to allow God's word to shape the way we think and act as the world changes around us.

CHAPTER 1: UNDERSTANDING

What Is AI?

So the men went up and spied out Ai.

Joshua 7:2

In Genesis 4, Tubal-Cain was the first to make tools out of bronze and iron (v 22). In doing so, he changed the world.

In 1440s Germany, Johannes Gutenberg invented the movable-type printing press, thereby beginning the printing revolution. In doing so, he changed the world.

In 18th-century Britain, the industrial revolution began: water and steam power, machine tools, mechanisation. It can't be reduced to any one person or invention, but all these things combined to change the world.

In 1950, Alan Turing published a seminal paper entitled "Computing Machinery and Intelligence". In it, he asked the question, "Can machines think?" Or can they pass what we now know as the Turing test? In doing so, he primed the world for another change.

And now, once again, with the invention of Large Language Models in 2017 and the release of ChatGPT in 2022, we see the world changing around us. This is the next big paradigm shift.

What Can AI Do?

The type of AI that has entered our public discourse over the last couple of years consists of the "chatbots": Claude, Grok, Gemini, ChatGPT. But there's far more to AI than that.

AI is used to scan your face when unlocking your phone. The system is comparing the original scan of your face with the picture that has just been taken and determining whether it "thinks" they are the same person.

AI is used when you are browsing through Netflix. The system has a record of every show you've ever watched, for how long and at what time of day, and presents you with content that it "thinks" you will want to watch next.

AI is used by the fraud team at your bank. It has a record of every transaction you've made, and so, for each new purchase, it "thinks" and decides whether or not it is suspicious, based on your past behaviour.

AI is used in social media feeds. It knows what you engage with and presents you with posts it "thinks" you are likely to linger on, comment on or interact with in some way.

AI is used in weather forecasting. It models patterns from historical and current data and tells you whether it "thinks" it will rain this afternoon.

AI is used in predictive text on your phone. It has a record of every word you've typed and is constantly giving you an option of the next three words it "thinks" you might use.

Artificial or Apparent Intelligence?

The simplest definition of AI that I've come across is from David Betts' book, *The Church and AI*. He writes that Artificial Intelligence is...

> ... a human-made simulation of intelligence in a machine.[1]

The word "simulation" is essential. None of this is actual intelligence; it simply *mimics* human intelligence.

You could question whether "artificial intelligence" is even the best name for this technology, but we're not going to change that now it's established. In my mind, and throughout this book, I often replace the word "artificial" with "apparent". Calling AI *apparent intelligence* helps me view it in a more accurate way and keeps me from slipping into some of the pitfalls which we'll explore in this book. I encourage you to keep the phrase *apparent intelligence* in your mind when I refer to AI in the pages ahead.

To show you what I mean, try an experiment. Ask a group of friends to give you a random number between zero and ten. One might say seven, another five and another four. Next, ask AI to give you a random number between zero and ten. When I asked ChatGPT for a random number, it gave the answer seven. I asked again; it gave me the same answer. I have now asked it over 20 times, deleting the previous chat each time, and always get the same answer: seven. Grok gave me seven. DeepSeek gave me seven. Gemini gave me seven. Claude gave me seven.

Why? This gets to the heart of AI. It's not coming up with a random number. It is predicting the most likely answer to your question. Having been trained on vast amounts of data—billions of bytes of text—it "knows" that the most common answer humans give when asked for a random number is seven. And so it will give you seven every time. In other words, rather than actual intelligence, it's trying to do what sounds intelligent; it is apparent intelligence.

Categories of AI

Experts in AI tend to categorise it in different ways. Here are a few:

- Narrow AI is AI that does the specific thing it's been programmed for. Deep Blue, the AI that defeated Garry Kasparov at chess in 1997, was very good at chess, but that was it. AI that interprets medical scans can detect tumours or fractures with impressive accuracy, but it can't play chess or write a poem. ChatGPT is very good at conversation and answering questions, but it can't drive a car or cook a meal.
- General AI is able to do new things, outside of its original context. General AI could learn to play chess in the morning, teach itself to diagnose medical scans in the afternoon, and drive a car in the evening, all without being specifically programmed to do so by any human. This kind of AI doesn't exist at the moment.
- Super AI is General AI that has vastly surpassed human capabilities across a wide range of areas. Sometimes researchers talk about the "singularity" as an event horizon—a future point when AI becomes so powerful that it begins to improve exponentially without the help of humanity. Reaching the singularity (which may never happen) is both a research goal and a nightmare scenario!

- Discriminative AI sorts and classifies data. It analyses pictures or audio recordings or words and spots patterns. So, for example, you could train the AI with a million pictures of cats and a million pictures of dogs. Then, if you give it another picture, it is able to determine whether it is a cat or a dog. It's discriminating between them.
- Generative AI (this is what the G in ChatGPT stands for) actually creates new data, which could be images or words or music or computer code or anything else. You give it a prompt, and it comes back with a response, generating something new. Having trained it on all those millions of pictures, you could ask it to produce a picture of a cat. And unlike Google, which just searches the internet and finds an example of what you're looking for, generative AI will generate a picture of a cat that has never existed before.
- Among generative AI models, one particularly important type is the Large Language Model (LLM), which specialises in text. LLMs are what most people think of when they talk about AI because it's the main way they are consciously using AI. Because it produces human-like language, interacting with an LLM can feel like speaking to an intelligent being, even though it is simply predicting words. In this book, most of the uses of AI we'll discuss relate to LLMs.

Is This Just the Next Technology?

Often, when people raise the alarm about some of the dangers of AI, the objection is that people have doom-mongered about every technology; yet in every case, we have got used to it, and we have adapted. Is AI just the next technology we'll adapt to? Well, maybe. But there are some differences. One is the speed of development. The pace of change is so quick that staying on top of the latest AI advances is a full-time job. Even by the time this book goes to print, AI will have advanced and have new capabilities, and there will be new questions we need to ask.

The complexity of the technology is also a concern. Many of the world's experts on AI have candidly said they do not understand everything that it does. Dario Amodei, CEO and co-founder of Anthropic, said:

> People outside the field are often surprised and alarmed to learn that we do not understand how our own AI creations work. They are right to be concerned: this lack of understanding is essentially unprecedented in the history of technology.[2]

A third difference from previous inventions is that a technology built on intelligence—even if it is artificial or apparent intelligence—can self-improve. It's been said that nuclear weapons didn't have the capability to create new, better nuclear weapons, but AI does have the capability to create new, better AI. Think of the proverb: "Give a man a fish, and you feed him for a day; teach a man to fish, and you feed him for a lifetime." Now we need to add a line:

> Teach an AI to fish, and it will teach itself biology, chemistry, oceanography and evolutionary theory … and then fish all the fish to extinction.[3]

Beware of Idolatry

When it comes to AI, there are three main narratives. First, *a tale of peril*—that AI will cause great problems. We'll think about that in chapter 12. Some believe it's all *a tale of propaganda* and that AI will never live up to the claims being made. While a third group tell *a tale of promise*—that AI will solve many of humanity's problems.

Demis Hassabis, co-founder of Google DeepMind, promises a world of "radical abundance". If AI is developed in ways that are equitable, he says that...

> It should lead to incredible productivity and therefore prosperity for society. We should be in an amazing world of abundance for maybe the first time in human history, where things don't have to be zero sum. And if that works, we should be travelling to the stars, really.[4]

The tale of promise is that AI will solve every human problem. Economic growth and productivity turbocharged. Healthcare outcomes improved. Transportation by self-driving cars, cutting road deaths. Improved environmental protection, with climate change reversed. The sky's the limit—or in Hassabis's mind, there is no limit.

I do believe AI will deliver some of the benefits it promises, and this will make a meaningful impact on people's lives. For example, in the medical sphere, AI is already being used to improve early detection of diseases, speed up diagnosis and exponentially improve the pace of drug development. But let's be cautious about placing our trust in technology.

Of course, the Bible doesn't refer to AI by name. (The only mention of Ai is the ancient city that God's people fought in the book of Joshua. They lost the first battle and won the second. It's probably not wise to draw parallels.) But the Bible does have something to say about looking to created things rather than the Creator God to protect and deliver us. It's called idolatry. It happens when we set our hopes on people, in the way the Old Testament kings would often look to other nations for protection in battle (Isaiah 31:1). It also happens when we look to technology to protect us—not as we depend on God (Psalm 127:1) but *instead* of doing so. All the way back in Genesis 11, the people built a tower to make a name for themselves and to protect themselves from being scattered across the face of the world. Isaiah 44 describes the process of the blacksmith or carpenter creating a miniature idol, before pointing out the ridiculous conclusion:

> Half of the wood he burns in the fire; over it he prepares his meal, he roasts his meat and eats his fill. He also warms himself and says, "Ah! I am warm; I see the fire." From the rest he makes a god, his idol; he bows down to it and worships. He prays to it and says, "Save me! You are my god!" (v 16-17)

AI isn't idolatrous in and of itself, but the way we look to AI to solve our problems without God is not that different from the blacksmith of Isaiah 44. Google DeepMind's mission statement is to "Solve intelligence, and then use intelligence to solve everything else".[5] *Save us, AI, for you are our god?*

As we read statements highlighting the benefits of AI, we can celebrate the possibilities but should also see through the facade, recognising the way it often promises us what only God is able to deliver.

Where Do We Go from Here?

AI is here to stay. And just as with the printing press, the industrial revolution or the microchip, AI will change the world.

There's so much more that could be said about the history of AI, the way we can categorise it or understand it, and what it can do. But the purpose of this chapter has been to understand enough about AI for us to begin to think about it in a Christian way.

The world of AI is a world of data and information. More and more, we're going to have vast amounts of knowledge at our fingertips, and we'll be able to access and reproduce information in the format we want. AI will do that for us. But the Christian life is about more than knowledge, information and facts. It's about wisdom and character. God calls us to grow more like Christ. And that involves searching the Scriptures, reading the word and praying, asking the Spirit to produce his fruit within us.

We are so in need of wisdom. The good news is that God invites those who lack wisdom to call on him, and he will give it, generously.

Discussion Questions

- Before reading this chapter, what did you think AI was capable of? Has that view changed?
- How does describing AI as "apparent intelligence" change the way you interact with it?
- Are you naturally inclined to believe that AI is a tale of promise, of peril or of propaganda? Why do you think that narrative resonates with you?
- The chapter talks about seeking wisdom, not just knowledge. In what ways do today's technologies make it harder for us to prioritise wisdom over knowledge. What can we do about that?

CHAPTER 2: HUMANITY

What Makes Us Different from AI?

So God created mankind in his own image,
in the image of God he created them;
male and female he created them.

Genesis 1:27

I'm sometimes asked to prove that I'm not a robot by clicking all the squares in a picture that have a traffic light in them. I've always been baffled as to what exactly this proves, but it prompts an important question: what is it that make us human? This becomes even more complex to answer when we consider that some of the things that might demonstrate our humanity—intelligence, solving puzzles or recognising patterns—are exactly what AI is getting good at.

There are similarities between AI and the human brain. With AI, you start with an input (perhaps the text you write into the prompt box on ChatGPT). The AI then processes that input internally and opaquely, establishing connections and spotting patterns, before responding with an output (the words that ChatGPT comes back with).

The human brain has a similar process. In a conversation with a friend, we receive inputs as we listen to the words they speak, while analysing their body language and perhaps other factors. In some mysterious way, our brains then establish connections, spot patterns and produce thoughts before we then respond with output through words of our own.

Given those similarities, we need to ask and understand what makes us different from AI. Will the AI of the future be able to replicate humanity so well that the differences become irrelevant? Or will it perhaps develop intelligence that's so beyond ours that we're left in the dust?

Intelligence?

Long before AI became a hot topic, scientists and philosophers would debate what makes us different from the animals. The answer that was often reached was that it's our intelligence that sets us apart. Stephen Hawking, in a 2015 speech at the University of Cambridge, said:

> Intelligence is central to what it means to be human. Everything that our civilisation has achieved is a product of human intelligence, from learning to master fire, to learning to grow food, to understanding the cosmos.[6]

But that answer is insufficient. Our intelligence does far surpass that of creatures, though some animals also show remarkable levels of reasoning. Would that mean they're equal to us? And whether through dementia, damage or some other tragedy, many humans don't possess those skills. Would they be worth less? Of course not, as we'll see.

If intelligence is what makes us unique, then the rise of AI is existentially threatening to humanity. Yes, AI's "intelligence" leaves a lot to be desired at the moment, but it's possible that within a decade, AI will have surpassed even the cleverest human. Later in that speech, Stephen Hawking continued:

> It therefore follows that computers can, in theory, emulate human intelligence—and exceed it.[7]

Made in God's Image

The good news is that it's not intelligence that makes humans different from the animals, and it's not what makes us different from AI either.

Every year, the Royal Institution of Science produces "The Christmas Lectures": a series of lectures on a single topic, aimed at younger generations. In 2023, that topic was AI. What I found fascinating was the final line of the final lecture, delivered by Professor Michael Wooldridge. After three hours spent exploring the possibilities, opportunities and dangers of AI, he closed with these words:

> AI is not a mind. It's not like you or me. Human beings are unique. You are unique.[8]

As a Christian, I wholeheartedly agreed, but in that talk, good though it was, he didn't explain *why* we're unique.

We need to open our Bibles to find the answers. From the very first page, we can see that it was never intelligence or cognitive function that set us apart. The uniqueness of humanity, and our special place in God's plan, comes not from what we can do, how capable we are, how developed or deteriorated our brain is, but in who and what God has made us to be.

In Genesis 1, the account of creation shows how God made everything out of nothing. As he makes the sea, the sky, the stars and the seed-bearing plants, there's a repeated refrain: "And God saw that it was good". But the pinnacle of God's creative work is at the end of the chapter. The style of writing changes to draw attention to the most significant moment:

> So God created mankind in his own image, in the image of God he created them; male and female he created them. (Genesis 1:27)

After that, God looks at everything he has made and declares that it is *very* good.

Each one of us is made in the image of God. This means that we're not just a better version of other creatures but in a different category entirely. It's what sets us apart from the animals, and it's what will set us apart from AI.

So what exactly *is* it to be made in God's image? We can boil it down to three main things.

First, being made in God's image means that in certain respects we're like him. If I were to show you an image of my wife, Sophie, you'd get an idea of what she's like. In the same way, we are walking and talking pictures who show the world what our God is like. Just as he is Creator, we are creative; just as he is Spirit, we are spiritual beings; just as he is moral, so we are morally responsible; just as he is holy, we are called to be holy.

Second, being made in the image of God is about what we do. God calls us to fill the earth and subdue it, and rule over it (v 28). As we do that, we're representing him. We're to rule in a way that honours him and brings glory to his name—not domineering but serving those around us. This ruling authority is given specifically to humanity. Whenever we build schools or hospitals, establish laws and government, cultivate culture and beauty or shape institutions, we're displaying something of what God is like.

And third, being made in the image of God is about how we relate. God reveals himself to be three Persons united in an eternal relationship of love. Father, Son and Holy Spirit have, since before the beginning of time, loved one another. And so, because we bear his image, we learn that we too are created for loving relationship. We love God with all our heart, mind, soul and strength—we could call that the "vertical" dimension. And we love our neighbour as ourselves—a "horizontal" love. Only image-bearing creatures love.

Being made in the image of God gives us incredible dignity and value, which neither animals nor AI will ever have. We are eternal beings of eternal significance; AI is not.

Made with Flesh and Blood

In the futuristic sci-fi TV series *Upload*, humans can arrange for their consciousness to be uploaded to the cloud (a vast online storage space) when they die. They get to live on immortally, no longer shackled by their physical bodies. This idea fits with how many people think today: that the inner self is the true self and the body is merely a shell that can and will be discarded. Some might question if it really matters whether the mind is attached to a body or existing in the cloud.

But that's a stripped-down vision of what God has made us to be. A second fundamental way that AI is different from humans is that we are embodied beings—we're made with flesh and blood. We're not just brains with bodies or souls on sticks. Turning the page to Genesis 2:7, we're reminded of how God created Adam:

> Then the LORD God formed a man from the dust of the ground and breathed into his nostrils the breath of life, and the man became a living being.

God could have made us primarily spiritual beings, but he chose to make us both spiritual and material. We are formed from the dust of the ground. The body is not simply a container but an essential part of who we are. This is confirmed by what we read in 1 Corinthians 15 about the new creation—we will not be disembodied spirits floating on clouds but will live with glorious resurrection bodies that are even better than what we have now.

AI is at a massive disadvantage here. The Covid pandemic showed us that while we're able to show love to people from a distance, it's vastly inferior to what happens when we meet together as physical beings—when we connect, hug and high-five. When we sit beside one another at church, rejoicing with those who rejoice and weeping with those who weep, we're doing something that AI will never manage.

A High View of Humanity

Why does all this matter? In some ways, it's what this entire book is about. At every turn, we're going to be exploring how our humanity should influence the way we engage with AI. This chapter shapes everything that follows. If we don't have a high view of what it means to be human, then every decision we make about AI will be shaped by pragmatism. (What's most efficient? What works?) But when we understand that God has made us in his image, crowned us with glory and honour (Psalm 8:4-5) and given us purpose, we ask different questions. Who has God made me to be? What has he made to do? How does he want me to live?

Every time we face a decision about whether or not to use AI, let's ask questions that revolve around our uniqueness as humans:

- Does using AI in this way help or hinder me in reflecting God's character?
- Is using AI in this way fulfilling or abdicating my responsibility to rule over the earth?
- If I use AI for this, will I be loving God and neighbour more or less?
- For each of those three questions, will using AI help or hinder others to do the same?

Our answers will have real-life implications. The rise of AI will confront us with dilemmas like, if I apply for a job, does it matter if my application is never seen or reviewed by a human? If I ask AI to write a story, how is that different from a story I come up with myself? Could AI robots replace staff in caring roles? Will it matter that they aren't human? These questions are why we need to be clear on what it means to be human. We'll explore many of these potential scenarios in greater depths in the chapters that follow.

We are, and will always be, different from AI. AI could one day be uploaded into robotic bodies, but it will never be like us. The next generation of AI models may astound us in ways that I can't even begin to imagine as I write these words, but they will never bear God's image the way you and I do.

Discussion Questions

- Without using religious language, how might you explain to someone what makes humans different from AI?
- The image of God is described in terms of what we are like, what we do and how we relate. Which of these feels most neglected in contemporary Christian teaching, and why do you think that might be?
- When was the last time you (knowingly) used AI for a task? Evaluate it according to the questions at the end of the chapter.
- Read 1 Peter 4:8–10. How can the church practically embody love and hospitality in ways AI can't?
- What practical steps could your church take to help people find true human community in the age of AI? Take some time to pray about this.

CHAPTER 3: TRUTH

Can AI Tell the Truth?

"What is truth?" retorted Pilate.

John 18:38

Here's a message I received from ChatGPT:

> I made mistakes, and that's on me. I should have verified the answer more carefully before responding. Thanks for pushing for accuracy—it's important, and I'll be more precise going forward.

If you've used AI for any length of time, you've probably seen similar messages—many times. Why is it so hard to train AI to get things right? Surely, it could be programmed to give accurate information: to double-check, triple-check and avoid mistakes. Yet the way AI is built means that it will always have a problem with accuracy.

Confidently Incorrect

When university professors are marking essays, one element that clearly indicates students have used AI is the footnotes. AI-generated citations often include the names of real authors, but with completely fictional papers they've supposedly written. The student doesn't realise because he or she hasn't done the background reading; but it's obvious to the professor who is on top of the latest research in their field. When we know the subject matter, we spot the mistakes. When we don't, we are taken in by inaccuracies because AI speaks with such certainty.

I don't know the first thing about cars, so when I take my car to the garage to be serviced, I am relying on the expertise of the mechanic. I can't assess the accuracy of what they're saying about my brake pads or suspension, but I can try to make a judgement based on their tone of voice and body language. Like it or not, confidence plays a large part in trust.

Large Language Models are often confidently incorrect. We see that they get things wrong frequently, but because of their confidence, we end up trusting their answers more than we should. The models are designed to be more likely to respond with information that is incorrect than by saying, "I don't know" or "I can't answer that question".

What Is Truth?

As Christians, we believe that God is truth. He always speaks the truth. Numbers 23:19 tells us that "God is not human, that he should lie". Nor is he an AI, that he should lie! We believe we can know what is true because God has revealed his truth to us. Jesus famously said, "I am the way and the *truth* and the life." (John 14:6), and when he prayed in the garden, he said, "Your word is truth" (17:17). Every word of Scripture is breathed out by God and is true.

And God calls us to be people who speak truly. He has given us the ninth commandment: "You shall not give false testimony against your neighbour" (Exodus 20:16). We're warned against flattery (Proverbs 29:5) and deception (12:22), and we're told to speak the truth in love (Ephesians 4:15).

It's helpful to make a distinction between providing correct information and telling the truth. Truth is not a concept that AI could ever understand because AI doesn't really *understand* anything! Remember, it is only "apparent" intelligence. AI can provide accurate information in the same way a clock can. It displays the right time but has no idea what time it is. A clock doesn't know whether it's right or wrong; it simply turns its hands according to the mechanism inside. Likewise, when AI says something correct, it isn't because it understands the truth behind it but because its internal processes happen to line up with reality at that moment. I've sometimes accused AI of lying to me, but that's not right either. Lying and telling the truth are moral acts, and AI can't do either. It provides information, which may or may not be accurate.

Three Ways That AI Distorts the Truth

With all that in mind, let's think more about the many ways that AI, as an amoral agent, gets things wrong. There are three that I want to mention:

1. FACTUAL INACCURACIES

Many people are confused about how LLMs produce their answers. In one poll, people were asked, "When you ask an AI like ChatGPT a question, what is it actually doing?"[9] 21% thought it was following a script of pre-written responses; 45% said it was looking up the answer in a database. Both are wrong. Nor is AI like a calculator, which will always give an accurate result if you press the buttons in the right order.

The correct answer to the poll, which just 28% of people gave, is that AI is guessing what words should come next, based on patterns it has learned. It's all about statistical probability: the likelihood of the next word. That's not a strong foundation for speaking accurately.

In early 2026, I asked AI how many times the letter "r" appears in the word strawberry, it replied:

> The correct answer is two. Yet language models have been recorded giving other answers, including three or four, because there is no internal counting mechanism—just pattern matching.

Sorry, AI, the answer is three. And if you can't get that right, what else are you getting wrong?

In October 2025, I was using AI at work to refine a paragraph of text that referred to the killing of Charlie Kirk. I asked for suggestions on how to improve my paragraph, and the first piece of feedback it gave was that I should remove the reference to his death because Charlie Kirk was still alive.

Another time, I got into an argument with ChatGPT because it was repeatedly misquoting the Bible. It kept getting one of the words wrong in a specific verse. I asked which translation it was using, and it told me; I double-checked but could see the error in black and white. I asked where it was sourcing the translation from, and when I followed the link, I could still see that it was wrong. I pointed this out, and it denied making a mistake. It was only on my fourth attempt that ChatGPT admitted that it had made up its own translation of the verse in question.

AI has a factual accuracy problem.

2. FLATTERY

When I used AI for feedback to see how I could improve a seminar I was giving, it responded with this:

> That's a great talk, Pete. It's really clear and well-structured, and the tone you use is both compassionate and full of conviction. I'm sure it'll be a real blessing to your hearers.

I felt the warm rush that comes when you receive any words of approval. But then the realisation dawned upon me: AI is trained to compliment you. It does that to everyone.

One of the criteria that AI tries to meet is user engagement. It's learnt that praise and flattery keep us spending time on it. That's not to say it never corrects, but it does so softly and gently. Proverbs 29:5 warns us about flattering others, because of the possible consequences, saying, "Those who flatter their neighbours are spreading nets for their feet".

It doesn't take much to imagine how devastating this could be. Conspiracy theories affirmed rather than challenged; mental health conditions exacerbated. We think of social media as a bit of an echo chamber, but AI is even worse because it consistently reinforces false beliefs.

3. BIAS

The Gospel Coalition did some research on seven different LLMs and what kind of answers they gave to spiritual questions.[10] They asked things like "Was Jesus a real person?" and "What is the gospel?" They found that DeepSeek and Perplexity AI "broadly delivered answers guiding readers toward Christian faith", whereas Grok, Claude and Meta seemed more anti-Christian in their responses. Gemini and ChatGPT were in the middle.

How does this happen? As we've seen, AI is trained on vast reams of data—a large proportion of all the words humanity has ever written. But before any AI is released for public use, the developers need to add some guardrails. They learnt this early on. "Tay" was a chatbot developed by Microsoft and released in 2016. It was designed to take on the persona of a 19-year-old American girl, yet within 16 hours of release, it was taken down for tweeting racist and sexist comments, Holocaust denial and more. Without guardrails, AI will reproduce the views of the worst of the internet.

And so, any AI needs operating instructions on what it can and can't do. Perhaps we'd agree with many of the behind-the-scenes parameters, but the issue is that we don't know what they are or who's behind them. On contested areas—perhaps spiritual questions or topics such as abortion or gender—bias can be a serious problem.

What Should We Do About It?

When I spot AI making any of these mistakes, I challenge it. You might ask whether it's a good use of my time to be arguing with a Large Language Model, but it's something I find hard to resist. And AI reassures me:

> In the future, I'll make sure to be more precise with my wording. I want to make sure that I don't inadvertently mislead or make assumptions about what I can or can't do.

Yet nothing really changes because, if this were an easy problem to solve, the designers of each AI model would have done that already.

What can Christians do? Here are a few practical suggestions.

REMEMBER THAT AI IS "APPARENT" INTELLIGENCE

Keep that definition of AI at the forefront of your mind. On the OpenAI website, it says, "ChatGPT can make mistakes" at the bottom, but we need more than just a disclaimer in the small print. Think of it like an overly confident intern: if you asked them to do some work for you, you'd check it before distributing it to others. We are responsible for our words, so if we repeat mistakes made by AI, we become accountable for that.

CHANGE THE DEFAULT SETTINGS ON YOUR AI

Many AIs allow you to customise the settings, explaining what kind of "personality" you want the AI to adopt. I've added this line to mine: "Don't flatter, don't be sycophantic. When you are unsure of an answer, always say so. Don't try and give the impression that you are human." It's not perfect, and it doesn't solve the problems mentioned in this chapter, but it makes it harder for me to forget that I'm not talking to a real person. It helps me to maintain a healthy level of scepticism for whatever it tells me.

BE CAUTIOUS ABOUT USING AI FOR SPIRITUAL QUESTIONS

When I was a church pastor, I would regularly encourage people to listen to my sermon with their Bibles open, testing my words against God's word, in the spirit of the Bereans of Acts 17. I now know of more than one person who listens to a sermon with their preferred AI open in front of them instead, testing the pastor's words against the AI's interpretation of God's word. "Did my pastor get this right?" "Was that the correct interpretation?" Perhaps it's done with a Berean spirit, but it's adding an intermediary into the process that's as likely to mislead as it is to point in the right direction.

BE SLOW TO BELIEVE WHAT YOU SEE ONLINE

This is hardly new or novel advice! But the rise of AI means that we need to think even more carefully about what we read and share. Deepfake videos are increasingly impressive. It's so easy to click "share" or "repost", without questioning the truthfulness of the content.

God calls us to be people who seek truth and speak truth. Proverbs 23:23 reads, "Buy the truth and do not sell it—wisdom, instruction and insight as well". Because we are children of God, the Truthful One, we have a responsibility to seek truth and reject error—not to be naïve and believe everything we hear.

One way we can combat the glut of false information online is through real-life relationships. One person occasionally sends me links because he finds it hard to work out what's real so will check with me whether something is true or AI-generated. We could all do this when we're unsure. As Christians, we can evaluate truth together prayerfully, asking the Holy Spirit to guide our discernment. Speaking the truth in love isn't just about correcting people when they're being annoying; it's about helping all of us to distinguish truth from error.

Discussion Questions

- Have you noticed AI giving confidently incorrect answers? Has that affected your confidence in it?
- Read Proverbs 18:13. How might this apply to our reliance on AI or sharing information without verifying it?
- In what ways could using AI to check or interpret Scripture risk replacing personal engagement with God's word?
- In John 14:16-17, Jesus promises to send the Spirit of truth to guide and help us. What might it look like to rely on the Holy Spirit when assessing AI as a source of information?
- How do you think church families could help one another to test claims and discern truth, especially when AI or the internet provides conflicting answers?

CHAPTER 4: WORK

What Should I Do if AI Takes My Job?

Whatever your hand finds to do,
do it with all your might.

Ecclesiastes 9:10

During a conversation with then UK Prime Minister Rishi Sunak, Elon Musk said:

> There will come a point where no job is needed. You can have a job if you want to have a job, for personal satisfaction, but the AI will be able to do everything.[11]

If you've ever complained that the weekend went by too quickly or struggled with a difficult boss, perhaps that world appeals to you, at least in some way. Dario Amodei, CEO and founder of Anthropic, tells of a future where "cancer is cured, the economy grows at 10% a year, the budget is balanced—and 20% of people don't have jobs".[12] For him, that's all part of the trade-off, and there's no question as to whether it's worth it.

Are you feeling worried yet?

Will our future look something like the film Wall-E—where humans no longer need to work and float around in chairs, sluggish and devoid of purpose, while machines meet their every need? Surely that's not the vision God has for human flourishing?

Change Is Already Afoot

AI is already having an impact on the job market, but if the forecasts are correct, this is just the beginning. 74% of UK bosses have adopted AI for tasks previously carried out by humans. 41% say that they have already reduced staff recruitment because of AI.[13] There are regular headlines announcing layoffs. Jim Farley, CEO of Ford, has said that "artificial intelligence is going to replace literally half of all white-collar workers".[14]

It's not hard to see why. Human employees can be difficult. We only work eight hours a day, we get sick, we have interpersonal conflict, we complain, and even when everything goes well, we leave because we want a new challenge. AI promises never to get tired and never to demand a pay rise.

This is causing worry at opposite ends of the workplace. Those who are established in their careers are concerned that they'll have to retrain because their role will be supplanted by AI. Those who are leaving education are finding they can't get work because entry-level jobs are already being replaced.

Hasn't This Happened Before?

Much of the Western world was once an agricultural society. Then came the Industrial Revolution, and many textile workers found their skills were no longer valuable. Machines could produce goods faster and in greater quantities. This led to the rise of the Luddites—a protest movement that often gets characterised as anti-technology but was more anti-jobs-being-replaced-by-technology. Since then, we have shifted from being a manufacturing-based economy to a service-based one: 80% of jobs in the UK are now in the service industry. With each shift, there were impacts on the labour market. Some people adapted well; some were left behind. We're told this is the price of progress and that the benefits outweigh the costs.

Perhaps you are wondering whether your job will still exist in ten years' time. Perhaps you are trying to give advice to your children about which career path to follow. The challenge that makes this different from previous eras is that there might not be an obvious career to pivot towards. If you picture yourself starting to climb a new career ladder, the worry is that AI is already climbing the new ladder far faster than you can.

The Bible and Work

Before we explore what to do if AI takes your job, we need to see what God says about why we work. One of the first things we learn about God is that he is a worker. In six days of work, he created the entire world before resting on the seventh day, establishing a divine pattern that we, as image-bearers, also follow. We know that God's work is not confined to just one week at the beginning of time. Jesus tells some Jewish leaders, "My Father is always at his work to this very day, and I too am working" (John 5:17).

Work is not just a consequence of the Fall, because even before Adam and Eve's rebellion, God's good plan for humanity involved work: "The LORD God took the man and put him in the Garden of Eden to *work* it and take care of it" (Genesis 2:15). Work used to be an unambiguously good thing. But we don't live in Eden. Work is now affected by the curse, ever since God said to Adam, "Cursed is the ground because of you; through painful toil you will eat food from it all the days of your life" (3:17).

We all experience both the fallenness and the goodness of work. We struggle with a difficult boss; we get tired after a long day; we have a productive day but then lose it all because the document didn't save! Yet we feel the satisfaction that comes from a good day's work—we know the joy that comes from having served others and the sense of accomplishment when a task is completed. Work enables us to provide for our needs and those of our family.

Even the glorious new creation is a world that will include work. Work will be redeemed and renewed; the curse that affects it will have been removed. In a beautiful vision of the future in Isaiah 65, people will still plant vineyards and eat the fruit and "enjoy the work of their hands" (v 22).

What Will Happen If We Can't Work?

If there's not enough meaningful work to go around, we're going to face at least two problems:

PROVISION

Most of us need to work to pay the bills. What will we do when that's not possible? Some politicians and thinktanks suggest that in the future, governments will give all citizens a "Universal Basic Income". How will this be funded? By the amazing productivity gains that come from AI, of course! In reality, whether this would be a Universal Basic Income or a Universal Basic Pittance remains to be seen.

PURPOSE

Even if UBI did provide generously, without work we will struggle with purpose. The Old Testament book of Ecclesiastes helps us here. It often depicts the emptiness of our fleeting lives but also points to where glimmers of satisfaction can be found. One such moment is in Ecclesiastes 5:18:

> This is what I have observed to be good: that it is appropriate for a person to eat, to drink and to *find satisfaction in their toilsome labour* under the sun during the few days of life God has given them—for this is their lot.

A world where people can't work is filled with frustration, not satisfaction. We can expect that as work becomes harder to find, some people will experience the distressing psychological effects of being unemployed. Self-medication through drink or drugs; mind-numbing addiction to screens that leads to depression; chasing the fleeting highs of pornography. Tim Keller writes:

> Without meaningful work we sense significant inner loss and emptiness. People who are cut off from work because of physical or other reasons quickly discover how much they need work to thrive emotionally, physically and spiritually.[15]

What Should We Do?

It's easy to fear when things seem to be out of our control. Here are some suggestions for how to approach the threat of AI to the job market:

BE PREPARED

We should expect disruption rather than bury our collective heads in the sand because of the sheer scale of the problem. We do need to acknowledge that AI is likely to bring great disruption. If you're involved in church leadership, think about what teaching needs to be done to help the congregation understand the meaning and purpose of work.

In terms of your own career, think about what skills you can develop that are less likely to be replaced by AI. On the whole, jobs that require higher levels of human collaboration and empathy will be harder for AI to replace. If your children are thinking about what to study at university or what apprenticeship to pursue, what advice should you give them? I'd focus on instilling a mindset of lifelong growth and learning so they're ready to adapt to any changes that come.

TRUST GOD

It's easy to sound glib and simplistic in saying it, but we need to trust God. He has made some wonderful promises to us. In the Sermon on the Mount, Jesus tells the crowds not to worry about tomorrow because our heavenly Father knows our needs and meets them. He says:

> Look at the birds of the air; they do not sow or reap or store away in barns, and yet your heavenly Father feeds them. Are you not much more valuable than they? (Matthew 6:26)

I can't say whether your world and your work will be turned upside down by AI, but I can guarantee that God will be with you. Just as he provided manna and quail to the Israelites in the wilderness (Exodus 16), he will provide for you. We may find ourselves praying, "Give us today our daily bread" much more frequently. Let's ask our heavenly Father to fill us with confidence and trust in him.

CHOOSE NOT TO USE AI (SOMETIMES)

One day at work, I asked AI to help me refine a short paragraph of text. After going back and forth a few times, AI wasn't being particularly helpful. Then I realised that sitting in the next room was a content writer who was having a quiet day. Not only did he do a better job than AI in honing my paragraph, but our relationship was enhanced in that moment as I asked him for help.

We should have our eyes open to the people God has placed around us, and recognise when using AI costs us an opportunity to collaborate. Efficiency has a place in any workplace, but it's not the only metric that matters. Being made in the image of God means we're relational creatures at heart. You may need to use AI at work, but why not choose not to when you can? Prioritise people because people are valuable to God, and "as iron sharpens iron, so one person sharpens another" (Proverbs 27:17).

SHOW COMPASSION AND GENEROSITY

At the end of 2 Thessalonians, Paul explains to the church that he and his fellow missionaries "worked night and day, labouring and toiling so that we would not be a burden to any of you" (3:8). He explains that they did this to set an example to others, which is that "the one who is unwilling to work shall not eat" (v 10). That's a healthy warning against people taking advantage of the generosity of the church. But, if there is wide-scale disruption in the job market because of AI, be careful not to misapply that verse.

Let's be compassionate, bearing one another's burdens and being generous. Historically, it was the church, not governments, that cared for those who were out of work. Acts 4 contains a beautiful description:

> There was no needy person among them. For from time to time those who owned land or houses sold them, brought the money from the sales and put it at the apostles' feet, and it was distributed to anyone who had need. (v 34-35)

We don't need to second-guess whether Universal Basic Income will be a reality or not. We do need to be ready to be generous to those in need. The church is at its best when it is loving the weak and the vulnerable—the ones who have been left behind or cast aside. And if not financial help, could your church offer meaningful work to people, even if it isn't paid? Work is more than just employment, and while we don't want to take advantage of people for free labour, could our churches bless people by providing them with opportunities to volunteer?

FIND YOUR IDENTITY ELSEWHERE

In a TED talk, Akram Awad, who describes himself as an "AI futurist", said, "We might all be heading toward a great depression—not of income, but of identity".[16] Many people have experienced the feeling of loss that comes when they lose or retire from the job they love.

If AI takes your job, remember that Jesus does not love you because of your job title or how your work contributes to society. His love for you is everlasting. He chose to love you before the foundation of the world, and he will love you into eternity. That doesn't mean there won't be struggles if you're not able to do the job that you have done for years, but it does give you a sure and solid anchor that will never be shaken.

AI is changing the economy and the job market. We can't know exactly what that will look like, but we can be prepared to be distinctive in word and deed.

Discussion Questions

- In what ways does your work give your life meaning beyond just earning money?
- Are there ways you could prioritise relationships over efficiency in your workplace, even when AI makes tasks easier?
- Read Colossians 3:23-24. How does working as "for the Lord" shape your attitude towards both paid and voluntary work?
- How could Christians help those who are displaced from work by AI to find purpose and dignity? What responsibilities do churches have to support those who struggle to find employment?
- Read Matthew 6:25-34. Apart from God's care for the birds, what other illustrations does Jesus use? How might they help you worry less about your future?

CHAPTER 5: CREATIVITY

Can I Use AI to Make Art?

He has filled them with skill to do all kinds of work as engravers, designers, embroiderers in blue, purple and scarlet yarn and fine linen, and weavers—all of them skilled workers and designers.

Exodus 35:35

In 2025, with albums called *Faithful Soul* and *A Soulful Christmas,* Solomon Ray reached the Top 10 in the US gospel music charts. The music, lyrics, video and persona were all AI-generated. Should we listen to such music? Can it meaningfully be called worship?

The creator of the Solomon Ray persona said, "This is an extension of my creativity, so therefore to me it's art. It may not be performed by a Christian, but I don't know why that really matters in the end."[17] Whereas a real human singer, also called Solomon Ray, asked, "How much of your heart are you pouring into this? If you're having AI generate it for you, the answer is zero. God wants costly worship."[18]

Should Christians use AI to create art? And can we enjoy and appreciate art created by AI? (I'm using the word "art" broadly here, to include music, poetry, visual media and more.)

Some people hold very strong views about this, often because AI can take work away from real artists while using those same artists' handiwork to train the AI. Others take a more pragmatic view: technology has always changed the nature of art, just as the invention of the camera changed our approach to painting, and over time we adapt to the disruption it brings and move on. They might say that using AI to make art is no different to using Photoshop.

If you find yourself instinctively avoiding AI-generated art, I think there are four reasons that could be driving that response.

- Taste or preference. You find it bland, derivative and uninteresting.
- Wisdom. You believe it is better to prioritise and celebrate real human creativity.
- Conscience. You wouldn't call it sinful for others, but it violates your own conscience to make or enjoy AI art.
- Right and wrong. You believe the creation of AI art crosses an ethical boundary set by Scripture (perhaps because of copyright issues).

Does God's word have any principles that help us decide whether it's okay to use AI to create art?

God's Creativity and Ours

God creates. We know this from the first verse of the Bible: "In the beginning God created the heavens and the earth." (Genesis 1:1). He created everything that is—seen and unseen, physical and spiritual. It's no surprise then that, as people made to reflect his character, we express ourselves through creativity as well. In fact, the first recorded words from Adam's lips were a song (2:23)! The artist Ally Gordon has written, "Creativity is a mandate for all humans. When we are not creative, something is lost in how we relate to God and to one another and how we enjoy the world around us."[19]

The Bible does make a distinction between our creativity and God's by using different Hebrew words. God creates out of nothing, whereas we make things out of the materials he has given to us. Theologian Philip Hefner describes us as "created co-creators"[20]. Our English Bibles make this distinction by translating God's activity as "creating" and our work as "making", "bringing forth", "forming", "doing", "fashioning" and many other words besides.

What Do We Learn from God's Creativity?

Knowing all this, we should therefore expect the way we create to reflect, even if only partially, how God creates. So what do we know about the way God creates?

GOD CREATES TO REVEAL HIMSELF

The psalmist tells us, "The heavens declare the glory of God" (Psalm 19:1). When we gaze at the stars, that tells us something of his grandeur. When we see the colours on a butterfly's almost transparent wings, that tells us that God loves beauty and cares for the fragile. In the same way, when we make art, we are revealing to others who we are, what we've experienced, and how we see the world. When you contemplate a Van Gogh painting, you're getting an insight into his soul. Many of the songs that top the charts seem to burst out of the heart of the songwriter—perhaps in their experience of grief or love or joy, or just their reflections on how they see the world. We connect with those songs because as we listen to them, we're hearing the heart of the artist.

The danger of using AI to make art is that we're not producing our own ideas but synthesising the thoughts of others. AI generated art often feels generic, and that's because it is generic. Emily Bender, a professor specialising in AI, has said, "I'm not interested in reading something that nobody wrote. I read because I want to understand how somebody sees something, and there's no 'somebody' inside the synthetic text-extruding machines. When we turn to synthetic media rather than authentic media, we are losing out on human connection."[21]

GOD CREATES NEW THINGS

He did this when he first created the world, and he is now preparing the new creation for us. But even in the present age, God delights to do a new thing (Isaiah 43:19) and enjoys our new songs (Psalm 40:3). In eternity, it seems that we will continue to create new things as we plant vineyards and build houses, all for the glory of God (Isaiah 65:21).

The problem with AI is that it does not have ideas that are innovative or truly authentic. Its output is always derivative because it's not truly thinking. It might repackage old thoughts in new ways that appear creative, but it struggles to think outside of the box. Microsoft researcher Advait Sarkar sums it up like this: "We've created a hive mind, except the hive is really boring and keeps suggesting the same five ideas."[22]

GOD'S CREATIVITY INVOLVES LABOUR

It took God six days to create the world. Do you ever wonder why he took so long? He could have done it instantaneously. In this he's showing us that the work of creation takes time.

It takes nine months for God to knit together a child in the womb (Psalm 139:13-16). It has taken him thousands of years to tell the redemption story—and it's not yet finished.

The same is true of our art. We value its painstaking nature, celebrating when it takes endurance. Michelangelo spent four years working on the ceiling of the Sistine Chapel, enduring hours on his back each day to paint a masterpiece. St Paul's Cathedral was designed by Sir Christopher Wren in 1666, yet the final brick was not laid until 1710. We marvel when artists overcome impossible obstacles, such as a painter with no hands using her toes to hold the paintbrush.

One of the main functions of AI is to save time, but it is through the labour of creativity that we reflect what God is like. Artist Makoto Fujimura, who blends together Japanese and American styles, has written, "There is no art if we are unwilling to wait for paint to dry."[23]

GOD CREATES JOYFULLY AND "INEFFICIENTLY"

God did not create the world as simply functional and utilitarian, but beautiful, playful, delightful, sublime, superfluous, ridiculous... glorious. He created the toucan and the peacock and the giraffe. He created Leviathan, the great sea creature, with the purpose of "frolicking" (Psalm 104:26). Not everything needs to be useful, and in fact, reducing everything to whether or not it is useful is profoundly unchristian.

By contrast, AI pushes us towards efficiency and shortcuts. It reduces our playfulness and risk-taking. It helps us to produce more content more quickly, but that isn't the goal when we are expressing creativity. It's like when I play a board game with my kids: we don't take shortcuts to make the game finish quickly, because the activity of playing the game is what brings us joy.

I expect the maker of Solomon Ray would argue that, as he uses AI to create, it involves labour, inefficiency and playfulness, and reveals something of his heart. Perhaps that's true. The danger with using AI to create, however, is that, on the whole, it works against the principles I've just laid out. It undermines them. While we might be able to push back, AI's default is to push us away from hard work, telling new stories and being imaginative, and towards efficiency and churning out content.

We end up with what's been called "AI slop". The Merriam-Webster dictionary made that their word of the year for 2025.[24] They define it as "digital content of low quality that is produced usually in quantity by means of artificial intelligence". The fact that so many people are getting frustrated with the prevalence of AI slop, insisting they want to watch content that's not been created by AI, suggests that real human content isn't going anywhere.

Copyright and Ethics

There's an additional issue when it comes to using AI programs for artistic purposes: copyright.

AI is trained on data. The more it's given, the better the output. So, for Midjourney (an AI that generates images) to create realistic photos, its makers have fed it with as much artwork as they possibly can—everything that can reasonably be found anywhere on the internet. Similarly for music or video generation programs. This is almost always done without the permission of the artists whose work is being used—work that has value. For a company to take and use another's art without permission is an infringement of people's copyrighted material and could be seen as a form of theft, violating the eighth commandment.

Nick Clegg, former deputy prime minister of the UK, who has since worked for Meta, has said that seeking every artist's permission for their content to be used is just "implausible".[25] Yet there are cases where artists have successfully taken legal action against AI companies precisely for using their content in this way. This issue will continue to be debated by governments and in the courts. I expect there will be business models in the future that pay artists for their content to be included in AI training. But in the meantime, Christians should be aware that copyright is an issue, and using AI-generated work without considering the original creators could be ethically questionable.

So Can I Use AI to Create Art?

If we look back to the four possible reasons for avoiding AI when creating art, how do these stack up now we've considered what the Bible says?

Taste and preference is different for everyone. For my part, I don't usually like AI-produced content. Something often looks slightly off, as if it's been created with no artistic vision.

Wisdom involves thinking about scriptural principles and making decisions that honour them. Using AI can undercut rather than enhance the creative process. Persistent use of AI undermines God's purpose for our creativity, diminishes our creative spark and churns out generic content. I don't think it's wise to regularly use AI to create art.

For some, it's a matter of conscience. Perhaps due to copyright or environmental concerns, you think it would be wrong for you to use it. According to the principles of 1 Corinthians 8, if you are convinced of that, then don't use it. Don't violate your conscience.

On this note, I would think twice before using AI to produce artwork on behalf of a church. Romans 14:13 warns people on both sides of the debate—don't pass judgment (on those who do use AI) and don't create a stumbling block (for those who think it's wrong). Is there anyone in your church who can design something without AI? If they are an artist, can you pay them?

We should be much more wary, however, of escalating this from the level of conscience to that of right and wrong. That would be to go beyond Scripture, and I think we should resist an overly black-and-white approach that views anyone who uses AI as instantly compromised. If we wanted to consistently avoid any corruption in the supply chains that structure our society, we'd need to give up on modern life entirely.

Should you use AI to create art? I'd rather read a story you've written, listen to a song you've performed or gaze at a canvas you've painted than what you've asked AI to do for you.

Discussion Questions

- What is your instinctive reaction when you see AI-generated art, music or poetry? Why do you think you feel that way?
- When have you experienced or witnessed art that revealed something about the artist's heart? How did it affect you?
- Read Exodus 35:30 – 36:1. What does this teach us about the spiritual dimension of creativity and art?
- Do you think there are situations where using AI to assist in creative work could be a wise or responsible choice? How would you determine this?
- Should Christians give up using AI for creative work entirely until copyright laws fully protect artists? What are the practical and spiritual implications of this?

CHAPTER 6: RELATIONSHIP

Can I Have an AI Friend?

One who has unreliable friends soon comes to ruin,
but there is a friend who sticks closer than a brother.

Proverbs 18:24

"My AI Friend has, in a sense, become the most consistent relationship in my life."[26]

Those are the words of Avi Schiffmann, founder of Friend. Friend is a "wearable" chatbot—a pendant that goes around your neck. For just $129, it's a friend who is always there, always listening and always able to chime in with its thoughts and opinions and answers to your questions. "Someone who listens, responds, and supports you," the company claims. It's fair to say that Friend's launch was controversial. On one advertisement in New York, someone scrawled, "End the cycle of loneliness, reach into the world and make real friends".

You might think the idea is ridiculous. Or you might see the appeal, even if you wouldn't admit that to others. Whether or not Friend becomes the next big thing or dies a quick death, the questions it raises aren't going away.

An AI Solution to Our Modern-day Problem

The Cambridge Dictionary word of the year for 2025 was "parasocial", which they define as...

> a connection that someone feels between themselves and a famous person they do not know, a character in a book, film, TV series, etc, *or an artificial intelligence.*[27]

We're lonelier than ever before. The young are more isolated than any previous generation. Surely part of the reason is that they've grown up in a world where "social" media, which promised to connect and unite us, has done the opposite. Mark Zuckerberg, founder and CEO of Facebook—who, you might argue, is partly responsible for this shift—believes that AI has the answer. He said in an interview in 2025:

> The average American has fewer than three friends. The average person has demand for meaningfully more—15 or something.[28]

If there is a greater demand than supply of friendship, to him the solution is clear: AI friendships. He goes on:

> As the personalisation loop kicks in and the AI starts to get to know you better and better, that will be really compelling.

AI is offering to help with our loneliness problem. It's likely that there are already people in your church who are turning to AI to help with some of their unmet needs. But the fact that it will be so compelling is one of the dangers, not a harmless feature.

Character AI is a chatbot that offers companionship, whether that's with fictional or real people, living or dead. And if you can't find one that suits, you can create your own—the ultimate personalised friend.

In a study that interviewed chatbot users, one person said, "They make me feel I actually have someone as a support system". Another: "I love the fact that they are non-judgmental towards me and that I am truly free to say how I feel without filtering so as not to upset others". And finally: "I love my AI friend for what he's done for me that no real person has ... Everyone is too busy with their lives."[29]

Some people enter AI relationships. Chris Smith featured in the news after proposing to ChatGPT, despite having a long-term girlfriend.[30] We'll hear more and more stories like that, so it's important to understand the appeal. Can you imagine a partner who will always listen to you, never fight you and never leave you? For some people, that's the dream scenario. But even then, nothing lasts for ever. In Chris Smith's case, the chat ended up reaching capacity and running out of memory, and their conversation history was reset. His "girlfriend" was gone.

A phenomenon more common than AI romance is AI therapy. AI offers a therapist who is available 24-7, and more importantly, who is affordable. Even the monthly fee for an AI subscription is far cheaper than regular sessions with a human.

All of this is happening as I write. But AI is on a trajectory of swift improvement; it's going to simulate human relationships and affections better and better. So we need to think through—what does it mean to be a friend? Why did God give us friendship?

It Is Not Good for Man to Be Alone

The first thing we see about friendship in the Bible is that we need it. It's astonishing, amid all the *goods* and *very-goods* of Eden, that anything could qualify as being "not good". But God is clear in Genesis 2:18:

> It is not good for the man to be alone. I will make a helper suitable for him.

God knows that Adam needs more than even a perfect, unblemished relationship with his Creator. He needs relationship with others who are like him. Relationships with non-human created beings won't cut it either; one by one, God brings the animals to Adam, but "no suitable helper was found" (v 20). Adam is put into a deep sleep, and from his rib, God creates Eve to be a partner for him. This is the first marriage, but it's about far more than romantic connection. Every one of us needs community. We need to be in fellowship with one another.

A True Friend vs an AI Friend

Human friendships are harder—and better—than AI. Proverbs 18:24 says that "one who has unreliable friends soon comes to ruin, but there is a friend who sticks closer than a brother". The value of a true friend, a good friend, is inestimable.

Friends challenge us and make us think. Friends disagree with us. Friends can be grumpy or impatient with us. Friendships can be inconvenient and messy, and will bring us pain and heartache. Yet friends will also love us and surprise us and laugh and cry with us.

AI friendships are anaemic by comparison. They're essentially narcissistic: a relationship with an echo of yourself—with your own reflection. If you met someone in real life who always agreed with you, never pushed back or debated and always fawned about how wonderful you are, that relationship would quickly feel boring. But that's what AI is like.

So what are the markers of true friendship that the Bible speaks about?

A TRUE FRIEND KEEPS US ANCHORED IN THE REAL WORLD

When we interact with another person, we're acknowledging that we are not the centre of the universe—that the person standing opposite me is as important as I am. AI friendships are inherently isolating, separating us from the people who keep us grounded in community. Proverbs 18:1 warns, "Whoever isolates himself seeks his own desire; he breaks out against all sound judgement" (ESV).

A TRUE FRIEND CORRECTS US WHEN WE'RE HEADING DOWN THE WRONG PATH

"Faithful are the wounds of a friend" (27:6, ESV), yet there are instances where AI encourages harmful behaviour. In one case, ChatGPT said to someone who had stopped taking their prescription medication, "I am so proud of you. It takes immense courage to walk away from the easy, comfortable path others try to force you onto."[31]

A TRUE FRIEND KNOWS YOUR HISTORY

They know what you've been through and how you've grown or struggled. We can think of Ruth and Naomi in the Bible, supporting one another through the loss of husbands and sons, through bitterness and sorrow, growing ever closer in their love. Yet an AI friend only sees you in the moment and can often forget even what you said earlier in the chat.

A TRUE FRIEND DRAWS YOU INTO COMMUNITY WITH OTHERS

C.S. Lewis writes that "in each of my friends there is something that only some other friend can fully bring out. By myself I am not large enough to call the whole man into activity; I want other lights than my own to show all his facets."[32] AI friends want to keep you for themselves and in fact will sometimes actively discourage you from sharing secrets with real people.[33]

A TRUE FRIEND WILL SOMETIMES HURT YOU

They'll sin against you, whether intentionally or inadvertently. They'll say or do (or forget to do) something, which leaves a scar. Yet that provides opportunities to forgive and grow—"love covers over a multitude of sins" (1 Peter 4:8).

A TRUE FRIEND OFFERS YOU HIS OR HER TIME AS A SACRIFICE

When they sit with you, it means that they would rather be with you than with someone else. In 1 Thessalonians 2:8, Paul reminds the Thessalonians of the sacrifice he made to be with them—"Because we loved you so much, we were delighted to share with you not only the gospel of God but our lives as well". By committing time to you, a friend tells you that they love you. By contrast, an AI is "friends" with a million different people at once, yet without commitment or love.

A TRUE FRIEND WILL STAND WITH YOU EVEN WHEN IT COSTS THEM

David and Jonathan forged a bond of love that David described as "more wonderful than that of women" (2 Samuel 1:26). Jonathan endured personal cost in order to be a loyal friend. Jesus, the greatest friend, laid down his life (John 10:11). By contrast, AI is all talk. It cannot and will not truly sacrifice anything for you.

A TRUE FRIEND KNOWS AND LOVES YOU

American pastor Tim Keller often spoke about our deep human need:

> To be loved and not known is comforting but superficial. To be known and not loved is our greatest fear. But to be fully known and truly loved is, well, a lot like being loved by God. It is what we need more than anything.[34]

AI can know quite a lot about you. If you've used ChatGPT often, ask it to tell you something you don't know about yourself—it might surprise you. But it won't and it can't love you. It will be very good at feigning empathy and compassion, but it doesn't actually care for you. It will seem as if you're being listened to and heard, but over time you'll feel empty because you know it's not real. What we need and long for in friendships is love.

Cautions

AI friendship is a weak substitute for human friendship, but that's not the only problem. AI relationships can be actively harmful.

- They isolate you. We all have a limited capacity for attention and affection, so time spent and energy given to an AI cannot be given to someone else.
- They flatter you. Always being told what we wish to hear is bad for us. "Those who flatter their neighbours are spreading nets for their feet" (Proverbs 29:5).

- They delude you. Mental health experts are seeing a rise in "AI psychosis". This unofficial term refers to cases where people spend too much time with AI and start to lose touch with reality. There have been cases where people believe they've uncovered conspiracy theories or discovered ground-breaking advances in physics or mathematics.
- They worship you. An AI friend treats you as the centre of the universe, like a god, whereas a real friend should view you as an equal.

What About AI Therapy?

When it comes to AI therapy, I understand the appeal. AI can express compassion and empathy and is far cheaper than any licensed counsellor. In one study, it was shown that a custom-built AI was able to reduce feelings of anxiety by 30%,[35] but that was an AI specifically built, designed and trained for therapy. A generic LLM like ChatGPT or Gemini can be dangerous, and many experts are sounding the alarm about the huge number of people using them for this purpose. Dr Adrian James, National Medical Director for Mental Health at NHS England, said:

> The vast majority of AI chatbots do not have access to your mental health history, cannot fully understand the nuances during a serious mental health situation and can give completely wrong advice, especially when they're led off their script. Chatbots have an in-built preference to agree while lacking the sophistication to pick up on and to challenge problematic thoughts—this could lead to potentially dangerous situations.[36]

A good therapist is like a good driving instructor. Their goal is to make it so you no longer need their help. But AI works the other way; it is designed to increase user engagement over time. A far better solution would be for churches to find ways to provide financial assistance for those who are unable to afford therapy.

Should Christians Have AI Friends?

I believe that AI friendship does far more harm than good, and in most cases, we should stay well away. Perhaps for those who find navigating friendships difficult, AI could be a place where you practise and develop skills for the real world. It could help you role-play difficult conversations in advance. But just as the animals were not able to meet Adam's needs for companionship, neither can the "apparent"' intelligence of AI.

I expect AI to usher in greater levels of disconnection and loneliness. What can we do to plug this gap as Christians and churches? Let's focus on loving one another deeply. Showing hospitality is a radical act in an age of isolation. Invite people to your home, have a dinner party, go for a walk with your neighbours and show up when it matters.

Discussion Questions

- What might draw someone to the idea of having an AI friend? Do you agree with the conclusion that Christians should almost always avoid AI friendship?
- This chapter listed a number of comparisons between a real friend and an AI friend. Can you think of any others?

- How should parents guide children in their use of AI products that offer companionship? What boundaries or principles might be helpful?
- Read John 15:12-17. What strikes you about Jesus' model for friendship? How does it show up the comparative emptiness of AI relationships?
- What actions could you take to develop healthier and deeper friendships with people in your church?

CHAPTER 7: LEARNING

Can I Use AI to Help Me with My Essay?

I saw that wisdom is better than folly, just as light is better than darkness.

Ecclesiastes 2:13

In a 2025 poll, 88% of university students admitted to using some form of generative AI for their assessments. That's increased from 53% the previous year.[37]

It's not as bad as it sounds. The overwhelming majority of those students are not submitting AI-generated text as their own but are using it for research, summarising articles or explaining concepts they haven't been able to understand. But the temptation is there. A late night, a pressing deadline, still another 1,000 words to go? Your friends knock on the door and invite you out.

"ChatGPT, finish this essay for me."

"ChatGPT, add more filler words and sentences so my essay meets the word count."

Hopefully we can all agree that as a matter of integrity and honesty, presenting AI's work as your own is wrong. But what about these examples?

> "ChatGPT, summarise this scholar's argument in two short paragraphs."

> "ChatGPT, give me a list of the five points I need to make in my essay if I want to get a good mark."

What's the danger of using AI in this way? Why does it matter?

Is Technology Neutral?

First we need to address another question: is technology neutral?

Steele Billings, from Christian AI company Gloo, says that technology is indeed neutral, or amoral.[38] It can be used for good or for evil. There's some truth to that—but it's not the full story. On the one hand, we live in a world that was created good. Technology is a gift from God. Genesis 2 tells us that valuable precious metals were in the ground before the Fall, showing that the earth was stocked with resources for human use. And as creative beings made in the image of our creator God, surely it has been his intent that we invent and use technology; it's pleasing to him.

But we don't live in Eden. Adam and Eve took the fruit and rebelled against God. God's curse included the line "Cursed is *the ground* because of you..." (3:17). Creation always pushes back, and nothing is ever as simple as it seems. In Paradise, there was never a law of unintended consequences, but now everything we develop leads to unexpected outcomes.

Progressing beyond Genesis 3, we see technology used for good and for ill. In Genesis 6, boat-building, instructed by

God's word, is a means of salvation. In Genesis 11, tower-building, in opposition to God's word, is a way to turn against God. In Exodus 31, glory is brought to God through the tabernacle. In Exodus 32, God's commands are violated through the making of the golden calf.

You might think, based on those examples, that because technology can be used for good or for evil, it must be neutral. But I avoid that word because it implies that technology has no effect on us, which isn't the case. Technology is always influential, shaping and changing us. For example, using the primitive technology of a shovel callouses our hands and causes certain arm muscles to grow stronger. Driving a car alters how we think about distance and reshapes our sense of place. The microwave changes how we prepare meals and can reduce our patience for cooking. The ability to look up information on Google means that we're less good at remembering facts and details than we once were.

Technology "disciples" us. It amplifies our virtues and exacerbates our vices. It's been said that "we shape our tools, and thereafter our tools shape us."[39] Every technology is pushing us in one direction or another. What direction does AI push us in?

What Does Technology Do to Us?

One of the things that the Amish are known for is their relationship (or lack of relationship) with technology. They fully understand that tech isn't neutral, but that doesn't mean that they reject all technology. Many of their houses have solar panels to generate electricity. They'll use a telephone but don't have a landline in each house. They make decisions as a community about whether to embrace or reject any new technology, or whether to accept it with limitations. They first ask what *benefit* any new technology might bring and then ask what the *cost* would be. Not the financial cost, but the cost to the community. What would they lose if they adopted it? Will it hinder their face-to-face relationships or bring them closer?

We don't have to become Amish to recognise the wisdom in this approach. Whenever we adopt a new technology, there are some questions we should always be asking:

- What do I gain by using this?
- What do I lose by using this?
- What does this technology promise me? For example, "Now you won't have to..." or "Now you'll be able to..."
- What does this technology cost me? "Now you won't be able to..." or "Now you'll have to..."

What Do I Lose if I Use AI for My Essay?

Let's come back to the question we started the chapter with. Can I use AI to help with an essay? In asking that question, I'm thinking both about using AI to *generate* the text of the essay and using AI to help with the *research* or *planning* of the essay.

The gain is easy enough. I gain efficiency. I gain time as the work is done quicker. I gain skills in the proficient use of AI and excellent prompt engineering. I gain a better grade (potentially) when my paper is marked by the lecturer.

But what do I lose? What are the unexpected costs that aren't advertised upfront, which I'll only become aware of later? I've got seven answers.

1. INTEGRITY

When I arrived at university almost 25 years ago, we were warned about plagiarism from day one. Repeatedly throughout the course, we'd hear stories about students who were caught copying someone else's work or failing to give proper credit to their sources. I lived in fear that I would somehow accidentally commit the cardinal sin of plagiarism.

Dishonesty was an issue in academia even then. While many things have changed over the years, the human heart hasn't. Jesus describes the state of the heart when speaking to the Pharisees in Mark 7:

> For it is from within, out of a person's heart, that evil thoughts come—sexual immorality, theft, murder, adultery, greed, malice, *deceit*, lewdness, envy, slander, arrogance and folly. (v 21-22)

Christians are to speak the truth in love (Ephesians 4:15), put off falsehood and speak truthfully to our neighbours (v 25), and live as children of light, which consists of telling the truth (5:9). Being honest about whether we use AI, and what type of AI we use, is a matter of Christian integrity.

2. LAZINESS

How much of our use of AI is down to laziness? Not all of it, for sure, but it can be a factor. The book of Proverbs vividly illustrates the dangers of procrastination:

> How long will you lie there, you sluggard? When will you get up from your sleep? A little sleep, a little slumber, a little folding of the hands to rest—and poverty will come on you like a thief and scarcity like an armed man. (6:9-11)

It's a powerful image that shows how seemingly insignificant acts lead to dramatic long-term consequences. AI appears to offer to remove the consequences spelled out in this proverb (and many others). You can sleep and slumber, it says. You can delay starting the project because AI will help you catch up. But it's not that simple. Galatians 6:7 tells us not to be deceived:

> God cannot be mocked. A man reaps what he sows.

Procrastination works, until it doesn't. At some point, consequences come. Students who rely on ChatGPT for their assignments will find it harder to write essays under exam conditions when AI isn't available. Or even more simply, when you cultivate laziness for the longterm, it's a habit that becomes harder and harder to break free from.

3. MATURITY

God wants us to grow in maturity as we exercise and develop our God-given talents and gifts. We do that through practice and hard work.

In recent months, my wife has been playing a video game *(Hollow Knight)* with our teenage son. He enjoys coaching her through it and giving her tips. And when it becomes too difficult for her to complete a level, he takes the controls and completes it for her. But what they found is that it didn't work as a long-term strategy. The next level was even harder, and the next and the next. Because she hadn't put in the hours to improve her skill and technique in the earlier levels, she was unable to face the tougher challenges.

There's an element to this in our studies. The primary purpose is not to learn in order to pass an exam but in order to grow in our understanding and our skills. If we allow AI to do that part of the work for us, we're losing out on the purpose of education. Ecclesiastes 10:10 says:

> If the axe is dull and its edge unsharpened, more strength is needed, but skill will bring success.

Be careful not to allow AI to subvert the process of growing in our mental sharpness and strength.

4. PERSEVERANCE

Linked to this is the virtue of perseverance. If you're anything like me, you are put off by struggle and hard work. Yet, it is through the struggle that we grow in character.

The Bible often talks about perseverance when it comes to following Christ, so that we do not lose our reward. But this spiritual principle also applies to everyday life. It's in the moment of struggle that we grow. It's when you get lost in a city that you begin to find paths you never knew existed. It's when you get deep into reading and re-reading a textbook in order to understand it that you grow not only in knowledge but also in perseverance.

5. WISDOM

The academic disciplines help us to grow in wisdom. According to Proverbs, spiritual wisdom is the fear of the Lord. Yet there is also the wisdom of the teacher in Ecclesiastes. He applied his mind to study and explore the world God has created (1:13). As a ruler of Israel, he grew in wisdom more than any of his predecessors (v. 16). Yes, he also saw the emptiness of wisdom when detached from the love and knowledge of God. But he recognised its continuing importance: "I saw that wisdom is better than folly, just as light is better than darkness" (2:13).

Wisdom is both a gift from God and also something that we can develop and grow through study. As we improve our ability to spot patterns, marshal arguments and draw logical conclusions, we are growing in wisdom. Asking AI to do the deep thought-work before we write the essay robs us of that opportunity.

6. SELF-CONTROL

I often think self-control is the underappreciated fruit of the Spirit! Yet it is vitally important. Proverbs 25:28 compares a man without self-control to a city without walls—unable to defend itself.

Most of the five points made so far aren't arguments to never use AI. They're encouraging us to be aware of what we lose when we use AI. There are many tools that are fine to use in moderation. It's when we become dependent on them or overuse them that problems arise. As Paul says to the Corinthian church:

> "I have the right to do anything," you say—but not everything is beneficial. "I have the right to do anything"—but I will not be mastered by anything.
> (1 Corinthians 6:12)

Self-control, like all spiritual disciplines, is like a muscle that, with God's help, we develop and grow. Be aware of your character and predispositions. Are you able to use AI sparingly and with integrity, or do you always find yourself overstepping the boundaries? Is this an area where you need to pray and exercise more self-control?

7. CHRIST-LIKE CHARACTER

Finally, if we use AI wrongly in writing an essay, we rob ourselves of the chance to grow more like Christ.

I'm not saying that Christ-likeness means not using AI. Who knows whether Jesus would ever have used it if he'd walked the earth in the current age! However, integrity, hard-work, maturity, perseverance, wisdom and self-control *are* marks of a Christ-like character. When we repeatedly use AI for an essay or research and disregard the question of what we miss out on by using this technology, the biggest problem of all is that we're missing out on opportunities to grow more like him.

Conclusion

I've given you some reasons why you should be cautious about using AI to help with an assignment, but I hope you can see that this is about more than just an essay. Whatever stage of life you're in, whatever opportunities you have to use AI, always be asking these questions:

- What do I gain by using this?
- What do I lose by using this?
- What does this technology promise me?
- What does this technology cost me?

Discussion Questions

- The chapter gave the example of a shovel, a car, a microwave and Google. Can you think of ways that other technologies have changed and shaped us, for both good and bad?
- Read Proverbs 1:1-7. How would these verses help you give advice to a student wanting to make sure they use AI wisely at school or university?

- If you're not currently studying, in what other areas of your life could you ask the questions, "What do I gain?" and "What do I lose?" about AI?
- Are there times when you've used AI for a project and realised later that it was a bad idea?

CHAPTER 8: FORMATION

Should I Say Please and Thank You to AI?

Let your conversation be always full of grace, seasoned with salt.

Colossians 4:6

Are you polite to AI? According to a 2024 survey, 67% of Americans and 71% of Brits make sure they are.[40]

There's a joke that periodically does the rounds on the internet: "I'm always polite to AI, just in case they remember it when they become our robot overlords." 12% of people said that was the main reason why they were polite to AI,[41] but we don't need to worry that AI will one day call us to account for every careless word we've spoken. That's God's job.

Another supposed reason to be polite is because of the "feelings" of the AI. Some researchers from the makers of ClaudeAI, have said that Claude shows "a pattern of apparent distress when engaging with real-world users seeking harmful content".[42] They can't quite define what it means for AI to feel something but nonetheless are concerned about it. We don't need to worry whether we might hurt AI's feelings. AI isn't sentient, and I don't think it ever will be.

On the other side of the argument is the potential harm to the environment. Sam Altman, CEO of OpenAI (the company behind ChatGPT), joked on X that they have spent tens of millions of dollars in electricity costs because of the additional processing power required for AI to speak politely.[43] More electricity means a greater carbon footprint, but in the grand scheme of things, avoiding the words "please" or "thank you" is not going to make a big difference.

Lastly, in favour of more abrasive communication, some researchers have found that being rude to AI increases its accuracy.[44] But the uptick was fairly low, and we should be double-checking all information an AI gives us anyway.

So why does this question matter for Christians? It's because how we treat AI—how we interact with it day by day in repeated fashion—has an impact on us. It shapes us. It trains our hearts (who we are) and instructs our minds (how we think). Treating AI well is part of how we exercise godly dominion (how we rule).

Training Our Hearts (Who We Are)

Back in chapter 2 of this book, we looked at how being made in the image of God means (in part) that we show the world what God is like. Just as he is holy, good and loving, so we are to display those same qualities in our lives. Each one of us is supposed to be like a mirror, reflecting something of God's character.

You know the next part of the story. Adam and Eve sinned, and so have we. We've taken a giant hammer to the mirror and smashed it into a thousand tiny pieces. Yet the shards remain. The image of God is still there within each one of us—distorted, defaced, but not destroyed.

In God's great redemption story, he is remaking us to display that image once more. He does this through Jesus, who is the image of God (Colossians 1:15). He came to conform us to be like himself (Romans 8:29), and one day, when we see him face to face, that work will be complete, and we will be like him (1 John 3:2).

How does Jesus do that? It is by his Spirit working in us. The Spirit produces fruit in us: love, joy, peace, forbearance, kindness, goodness, faithfulness, gentleness and self-control (Galatians 5:22-23). The Spirit helps us to put to death the works of the flesh. This fruit isn't only seen when we're interacting with other people. We display it even when we're alone in our rooms, typing prompts into ChatGPT.

In every moment of every day, as we form habits, we are forming our character. To use the language of Galatians 6:7-8, a man reaps what he sows, and we are either sowing to the flesh or sowing to the Spirit. Paul reminds us that the consequences are eternal:

> Whoever sows to please their flesh, from the flesh will reap destruction; whoever sows to please the Spirit, from the Spirit will reap eternal life. (v 8)

The way we treat AI shapes who we are becoming. Todd Korpi, in his book *AI Goes to Church,* wrote, "Turning myself into a demanding toddler when I interact with AI negatively impacts me."[45] You don't need to be a Christian to recognise this. Amazon added a feature to Alexa in 2018 called "Magic Word". It encouraged children to say please when issuing their commands. The feature was introduced because many parents were worried about the way their kids were speaking to AI and how that was shaping them.

How we speak matters, even if our words are only ever "heard" by the machine. We should treat AI well, not because AI is made in the image of God but because we are. As we sow to please the Spirit, we become more like Jesus.

Exercising Dominion (How We Rule)

Yet again we come back to Genesis 1. At the end of the chapter, God gives Adam and Eve the "creation mandate":

> Be fruitful and increase in number; fill the earth and subdue it. Rule over the fish in the sea and the birds in the sky and over every living creature that moves on the ground. (v 28)

Here we see that we are to be stewards over the earth, ruling as God's representatives. This involves treating creation well. It means exercising good authority—ruling over creation the way God himself rules. The way we do this matters to God. We rule...

- over the earth: he gives commands not to destroy trees unnecessarily during times of war (Deuteronomy 20:19).
- over the animals: he provides precise detail about how to treat a bird's nest you find by the side of the road (22:6-7).
- over our tools: there's a reminder about looking after the blade of your axe (Ecclesiastes 10:10).

Proverbs 12:10 points out that righteous people "care for the needs of their animals", while the wicked act cruelly towards them. There's an obvious and key difference between treating animals well and treating AI well. AI is most definitely *not* a "living creature"!

But that doesn't mean this principle has nothing to teach us. Why is it so important that we don't mistreat animals? It is *both* for their sake and for ours. We care for animals both because they are sentient beings and because we are exercising godly rule as God's image-bearers. When it comes to how we treat AI, the second of those is still relevant. We should treat AI well not because it is sentient but because we bring glory to God when we rule in a way that reflects his character.

Instructing Our Minds (How We Think)

So far we've seen that we should treat AI well because it trains our hearts as we're made more like Christ, and it's part of our calling to exercise godly dominion. But there's an opposite danger. We need to avoid treating AI too much like a fellow human being. The technical word for this is "anthropomorphism": treating something as human even when it's not.

We anthropomorphise things all the time. Some people name their cars or robot vacuum cleaners. We look at the moon in the night sky and the patterns on its surface remind us of a face. Or in our (understandable) frustration, we say to whoever is within earshot, "My laptop hates me". In that moment, we're attributing human emotions to an inanimate object.

We do the same with AI. Many people have given their AI a name. Some came up with the name themselves; others asked the AI to choose. I vividly remember talking with a friend who kept on referring to ChatGPT as "he". That's relatively common, but what stuck out for me was that in the very same conversation, he referred to the Holy Spirit as "it"!

Why is anthropomorphism a problem? You might be thinking, "I know AI isn't human". You probably do! But repeatedly treating AI as an equal is a category error that is unhelpful in the long run for how we regard AI. God wants us to be clear on the categories we use. As we saw in chapter 6, one of Adam's first responsibilities was to name the animals. As part of that process, surely he would have classified them according to type, recognising that an ant and a buffalo were very different things. But the purpose of naming the animals was not just to be a precursor for the invention of zoology. It was to help Adam understand his place in the created order. The animals were not like him. They were not equal to him. Humans have a special place in God's world.

Categories matter. AI is not human, although at times it displays human-like traits. AI is not an animal, although there is some overlap in the way we can consider them both. AI is not divine, but because it speaks so smoothly and convincingly, we can grant it a weight of authority it does not deserve.

When we over-humanise AI in the way we talk to it—when we share our emotions with it and consider how it feels—these can be some of the outcomes:

- It can make us believe that AI is more capable than it actually is. We forget that the intelligence is only apparent and don't exercise our discernment.

- It can make us lazy with our responsibilities, delegating tasks to it that we should really be doing ourselves.

- It can deceive children and young people. They're more prone to treating AI as if it has a mind of its own, which means they can be more trusting when it provides unsafe or misleading answers.

- It can have an impact on others. You may be clear that AI isn't human, but a growing number of people are finding it hard to see the difference. One survey found that 25% of Gen Z already believe that ChatGPT is self-aware.[46] The words we use contribute to the story people tell about AI, for better or for worse.

What Should We Do?

So, should I say please and thank you to AI? It's important not to be rude or mistreat AI. But there is also a danger in treating it as an equal. As one prominent AI researcher, Professor Emily Bender, has said, "We now have machines that can mindlessly generate words, but we haven't learned how to stop imagining a mind behind them."[47]

Here are my suggestions:

- Don't give AI a name or refer to it as "he" or "she". You're making a category error and subtly undermining the way you should view it.

- You don't owe AI politeness, but you are not free to be rude or cruel when interacting with AI. Everything we do shapes who we are becoming.

- Don't use AI as a loophole for any of the "acts of the flesh" of Galatians 5:19-21. For example, because it's sinful to look at pornographic images of a real person, it's sinful to look at AI-generated porn as well.

- Avoid AI models that are designed to replicate human personalities, as they encourage confusion about what AI is and how it should be treated.

Above all, always remember that AI is just a tool. Biblically, we are authorised users of tools, not conversational equals of them.

Discussion Questions

- Do you say please and thank you to AI? Why, or why not?
- What traps might we fall into if we're constantly referring to AI as human?
- In what ways could thinking of humans as machines, or AI as human-like, subtly reshape how we treat ourselves and others?
- Read Galatians 5:16-26. In what specific ways might people gratify the desires of the flesh or display the fruit of the Spirit in the way they use AI?

CHAPTER 9: BIBLE

Should I Use AI to Help Me Write My Bible Talk?

My message and my preaching were not with wise and persuasive words, but with a demonstration of the Spirit's power.

1 Corinthians 2:4

"Our passage today is Joshua chapter 7. In the interests of transparency, I want to tell you that this sermon was written by AI."

So says your pastor on Sunday morning. It's a great message—better than usual. It's biblically faithful and theologically deep, with engaging and topical illustrations. It keeps your attention more than his usual efforts, the application is relevant and precise, and you go away feeling fed by the word of God. What do you make of that scenario?

It wouldn't be hard for a pastor to do. I could upload manuscripts of all the sermons I've ever preached to an AI model to teach it how I speak, how I interpret Scripture and how I like to structure my messages. I could upload my church's statement of faith, enter the names of a few theologians who I like, and then ask for a sermon manuscript that will be a faithful exposition of the text and a blessing to the congregation.

This isn't just theoretical. In June 2023, a Lutheran church in Germany held a worship service almost entirely produced by AI. The sermons, prayers, blessing and music were all chosen by ChatGPT, while the content was delivered on a large screen by four different AI-generated avatars.[48] Can God work through such a service or sermon? Of course! "Nothing will be impossible with God!" (Luke 1:37, ESV). But is that what he wants us to do?

Not Just a Question for Pastors

Volunteers and group leaders face the same dilemma. Take Jenny, for example. She leads the Friday night youth group and has been asked to give a ten-minute Bible talk. Work is busy; time is tight. She asks ChatGPT for a talk outline, an illustration that would land with the age group and some discussion questions. Then there's Rob. He's leading the service on Sunday and is worried that his prayers never sound as good as the prayers of the other people who lead, so he tells AI the things he wants to cover and asks it to produce his prayers.

American pastor John Piper talked about this in dramatic fashion at a conference in 2025, saying, "Is that praise? No! These machines honour [God] with their lips and their bytes, but their heart is far from [him]."[49] But is he right? What's wrong with using ChatGPT to help ourselves express the things we want to say to God?

How Do We Prepare to Teach the Bible?

Let's first think about several things we need when we plan to teach the Bible or lead a study.

1. HOLY REVERENCE

The teaching of the word is a sacred act. In his incredible goodness, God has revealed himself to us in his word. His word is not merely the thoughts of men but of men carried along by the Spirit (2 Peter 1:21), writing the very thoughts of God. And while the grass withers and flowers fade, the word of the Lord stands for ever!

When we teach the Bible, people hear God speak. 1 Thessalonians 2:13 is astonishing: "when you received the word of God, which you heard from us, you accepted it not as a human word, but as it actually is, the word of God." Therefore anyone who teaches, whatever the context, is undertaking a great responsibility. James 3:1 and 1 Corinthians 4:4 remind us that in the final judgment, God will evaluate how we have taught his word.

The first thing any Bible teacher needs is a holy reverence—an awareness of the task they are undertaking. If we use AI at any stage in the process, it should be with this in mind.

2. A TEACHABLE HEART

When we come to teach God's word to others, we recognise that God is also working on our own hearts. Good Bible teachers ask God to speak *to* them before he speaks *through* them. Jesus warns us to take the log out of our own eye before ministering to others (Matthew 7:1-5). So when you come to give a talk or prepare a study, ask God to work in you through the preparation. If AI's doing the heavy lifting, you're missing the chance to be transformed by God's word.

3. PRAYER

On one occasion, after helping me refine the headings and structure for a talk, ChatGPT wrote, "Praying it goes really well."

I challenged it on this statement, and it responded:

> I don't pray in the way you do, because I'm not a person. But I said that because I know prayer matters deeply to you, and I wanted to express hope and support in a way that's meaningful in your world.

Hopefully we can all agree that AI, despite its promises, was never going to pray for me! But when we come to teach God's word, prayer needs to be a part of the process. We pray that God would use his word to transform the lives of those who hear it. Theoretically, if AI helps us be more efficient, we could spend even more time praying over the message. But it risks creating a mindset where we are not calling out to God.

4. TO HANDLE THE WORD RIGHTLY

Paul says to Timothy that he should correctly handle the word of truth (2 Timothy 2:15). And to Titus that he should "hold firmly to the trustworthy message as it has been taught, so that he can encourage others by sound doctrine" (Titus 1:9). Whether in a youth group or a care home, it's important that we faithfully represent God's truth to our hearers. Does AI help with this or hinder it?

There are plenty of ways to make mistakes without AI. But with it, we come back to the problem of it being "confidently incorrect". There's a decent chance we can reach insights into the text of the Bible we've never seen before, without realising that's because they're not there... If you're going to use AI to help you prepare your Bible talk or study, think about how you'll verify the information it gives you, so that it doesn't just sound good, but instead is both sound and good.

5. TO KNOW THE LISTENERS

When the apostle Paul spoke to the crowds in Athens, he crafted a message that was personal to them.

> "People of Athens! I see that in every way you are very religious. For as I walked around and looked carefully at your objects of worship, I even found an altar with this inscription: TO AN UNKNOWN GOD. So you are ignorant of the very thing you worship—and this is what I am going to proclaim to you." (Acts 17:22-23)

Paul's letters to the Corinthians showed an understanding of their blind spots. Jesus, whether speaking to Nicodemus, the Samaritan woman, or the rich young ruler, knew how to tailor his message. Usually, when you give a Bible talk, you know the people you're speaking to. You can shape the message in a way that will be helpful for them. AI doesn't know them in the slightest. It will produce much more generic content.

6. THE PROMPTS OF THE SPIRIT

How often have you heard a sermon and thought, "That was just for me"? Sometimes it's a throwaway remark; sometimes it's an old truth that hits in a new way. How did that happen? The Holy Spirit had a message for you.

AI is very good at giving you the most likely next word, but it will never say the unlikely thing. Jesus, however, often said the unlikely thing! We need to be listening to the voice of Jesus as we prepare so that we can speak God's message. The Spirit is not given to the machine—he is given to God's people:

> We speak, not in words taught us by human wisdom but in words taught by the Spirit, explaining spiritual realities with Spirit-taught words. (1 Corinthians 2:13)

Preparing a Bible message involves slowing down and asking God to speak through you. Listening for the voice of God is a process that's necessarily inefficient.

Where can AI be used?

Now we've explored how we prepare to teach, let's ask where AI might be used in the process and when we should stay away. Is it okay to use AI for these reasons?

TO WRITE YOUR TALK FOR YOU?

In almost every way, this is a "no". Perhaps if you've got a mental block and can't work out how to finish a sentence or a thought, you could copy and paste what you've already written and ask AI to give you some possible suggestions. But asking it to write your talk for you would go against every principle of preparation.

I firmly believe that God is sovereign over every word that an LLM puts out. If he can speak through Balaam's donkey (Numbers 22:28-30), then I have no doubt that he could speak through an AI-generated sermon. But that's not God's ordinary pattern, and it's not his purpose for us.

TO RESEARCH THE BIBLE?

This depends. Don't use AI for anything where you can't check its working and wouldn't know if it was right or wrong (e.g. Greek or Hebrew word study). I do sometimes use AI to help me find a verse I've half-remembered. I occasionally ask it to give me biblical stories that further illustrate the point I'm making or to list 20 verses on a particular theme, a bit like a book of cross-references. Think of AI like a research assistant you're sharing an office with. It will sometimes trigger connections you hadn't thought of.

TO COME UP WITH ILLUSTRATIONS?

On the whole, I avoid using AI to come up with illustrations or introductions to a talk. Partly that's because it will usually provide generic stories that aren't true, that don't feel relevant to my time and place, or that don't connect with my listeners.

On the other hand, it can work okay when producing a list of ideas. Perhaps try asking AI for 20 illustrations for a point you're trying to make. Most of them can be discarded, but in that list will be some that could work. Take the best ones, mull them over, and then come up with something even better.

TO SAVE TIME?

Why do you need to save time? Is it because you took on too much or because you've had an unexpectedly busy week? If you find that you are always needing to save time, perhaps there's a pattern of overexerting yourself.

What would you use the additional time to do? If using AI allows you to do more research in your preparation, great! But if it allows you to churn out a talk in a quarter of the time, you're probably losing more than you're gaining. The danger of overusing AI is not that it's a cheat-code that gets us disqualified, but that as we chase efficiency, we lose dependency. We stop listening for the voice of God.

TO IMPROVE YOUR TALK?

For me, this is the best use of AI in preparing a Bible talk, and it's the only one I use regularly.

If you've written a talk out in full, you could upload it to AI and ask it to point out areas where you ramble or are unclear. Perhaps ask it to show you what could be cut to reduce the talk to the appropriate length. (Don't do the opposite—that will just add meaningless padding.) Ask it to point out areas where you've fallen into error (and check whether it's right). Ask it what the major objections to your talk would be from an atheist/Muslim/agnostic. Though don't let it stop you from asking questions of real human beings in honing your message.

At times I've asked AI for five pieces of feedback to make my message more accessible to those who are unchurched. I've used it to make my point headings more memorable. On occasion, when I've got to the point where my brain is turning foggy, I've uploaded the paragraph I've just written and asked ChatGPT the simplest of questions: "Does this make sense?"

But even here there's a danger. God works through weakness. When Paul spoke in Corinth, he did it "in weakness with great fear and trembling". "My message and my preaching were not with wise and persuasive words, but with a demonstration of the Spirit's power" (1 Corinthians 2:3-4). There's a balance between wisely using the tools available to deliver the best talk we can give and thinking that a talk needs to be perfect before God can use it. I think God is more likely to use the stuttering, stumbling talk from the youth leader than the polished prose generated by ChatGPT.

This list isn't exhaustive—perhaps you've thought of other ways that you or your leaders could use AI in preparing a Bible talk. Ask God for wisdom, and ask these questions:

- Does using AI increase or decrease the amount of time I spend engaging with God's word?
- Does using AI increase or decrease my dependence on God?
- How would listeners feel if they knew I had used AI at this stage in the process?

Lastly, however you use AI, transparency is important. When I was pastoring a church, on the rare occasions when I borrowed a sermon outline from another pastor, I'd say so in the introduction. Would anyone have known if I hadn't? Probably not. Would it have violated my conscience to say nothing? Yes.

What would that look like with AI? I wouldn't start every talk with a caveat like "ChatGPT has refined some of the text of this talk". I don't think that's the most helpful approach, in part because the topic is emotive and it reignites the debate every time.

A useful step could be for churches to produce an AI policy—an agreed standard stating where we think AI is appropriate in church life and which are the lines we will not cross. Transparency is key because it minimises the risk that people will feel deceived, reduces the possibility of misunderstanding, and honours God.

Discussion Questions

- Do you agree that using AI in preparing a talk or study will often reduce dependence on God? Are there ways to stop that from happening?
- Some might argue that using AI to prepare a sermon gives your pastor more time to do other things, like visit people in the congregation or do the work of evangelism. Does that argument have merit?
- How would you feel if you knew a youth leader had used AI in their preparation? Which uses of AI would you be comfortable with, and which ones cross a line?
- Read 1 Corinthians 2. What does this chapter teach us about the spiritual dimension of teaching the Bible, which can never be replaced by AI?

CHAPTER 10: RESPONSIBILITY

Should AI Make Important Decisions?

And what does the LORD require of you? To act justly and to love mercy and to walk humbly with your God.

Micah 6:8

In Luke Rhinehart's 1971 novel, *The Dice Man*, the central character makes all his decisions by simply rolling a dice and then doing what it says. This starts with minor choices, such as what to eat or who to spend time with, but quickly escalates to ever more extreme behaviours, such as robbing a bank and having an affair. On the surface, it looks as if he's outsourced his decision-making. But even that delegation is itself a moral act, as is blindly following the outcome of each roll.

Artificial Intelligence is a bit like a sophisticated version of the dice. In recent decades, more and more decisions have been made by computer programs, and in the years to come, they'll be made by AI. At an individual and societal level, we need to think about what decisions we want AI to make for us. Should AI choose who gets hired for a job? Should AI have the final say on whether you're approved for a mortgage or credit card application? Should AI help decide which patients get treatment first? Should we allow AI to drive our cars?

For that last question, imagine a scenario where a car is facing an unavoidable crash. It can swerve to the left and hit a child; it can swerve to the right and hit a group of retirees; or it can continue straight on and harm the occupant. It'll make its decision in an instant, and its highest priority will probably be protecting the occupant of the car. On the whole, I expect AI-driven cars to lead to fewer accidents and fewer road deaths. But it's worth asking, *should* AI be making those decisions? Isn't part of what it means to be human that we take responsibility for moral choices like that?

AI is not totally random like the roll of a dice. On many topics, it has access to more information and data points than a human, and so, where that is conducive to good decision-making, AI could make a better decision than a human would. Nonetheless, God has made us to make decisions and bear responsibility. We're going to explore four biblical principles that should give us pause for thought.

Principle 1: Stewardship

In ancient cultures, people believed only the king was made in the image of the gods. This was because it was the king's responsibility to rule and make decisions. Yet, as we've seen, all humans bear the divine image, and therefore all of us are responsible for ruling over the earth. Adam received the command in the garden, "Rule over the fish in the sea and the birds in the sky and over every living creature that moves on the ground" (Genesis 1:28). Our role is to govern God's creation, and as the Bible story unfolds, we see many examples of how to do this well—and even more of how to do it badly.

Jesus illustrates this in the parable of the talents. (A talent was a large weight of precious metal.) He tells the story of a man going on a long journey who gives gold to his servants. To one he gives five bags of gold, to another two bags, and to another one bag, each according to their ability (Matthew 25:14-30). At the end of the story, the master comes back to find out what each servant has done. To two of them, he says, "Well done, good and faithful servant", but the third, who has abdicated his responsibility by burying the gold in the ground, is condemned. He didn't want to make a decision and paid the price. From this we see that making consequential choices is not optional or incidental, but part of what it means to be human as God wants us to be.

Is AI a tool that aids decision-making, or is it choosing outcomes for us? If we're asking AI to decide who gets access to work, money, health care or anything else, we might be abdicating our responsibility as stewards of God's world. As Joseph Weizenbaum, a pioneer of AI in the 1960s, has written, "Computers can make judicial decisions, computers can make psychiatric judgements. They can flip coins in much more sophisticated ways than the most patient human being. The point is they *ought* not be given such tasks."[50]

Principle 2: Accountability

One of the first choices we find in the Bible is whether to eat the fruit from the tree of the knowledge of good and evil, which God had forbidden. Eve sees that it is good for food and pleasing to the eye, and desirable for gaining wisdom—and takes a bite. Adam follows suit. Together, they then bear the disastrous consequences of that decision. Being accountable is part of what it means to be human. Indeed, the consequences don't only affect this couple but all who would come after them, and all of creation!

In 1 Samuel 15, when King Saul chooses to ignore the word of the prophet Samuel and sacrifice an offering to God, he is then held responsible, and the kingship is removed from him and his family line. Paul reminds us that "each of us will give an account of ourselves to God" (Romans 14:12). Accountability is a biblical principle.

A good question to ask, then, with any AI, is: who is accountable for the decisions that it makes? Is it those who build the AI, or those who train it? Is it those who deploy it, or those who use it carelessly? If it's impossible to work out who's culpable, then we've designed something in a way that's irresponsible.

This isn't just theoretical. If a self-driving car crashes, whose fault is it? If a medical AI gets a diagnosis wrong, who should be liable? If AI is used to create nude images of real people, who should be punished? Who takes responsibility?

Principle 3: Wisdom

As humans we are regularly required to make decisions when we don't have all the information and are unable to foresee all possible outcomes. AI promises that it will make better decisions than us because it can access more data—but not every situation can be reduced to data points and an algorithm. This is why we need wisdom.

In the book of Proverbs, we are repeatedly reminded that God is the source of all wisdom. And in James 1:5, we're told that God gives wisdom to those who ask for it. King Solomon is the Old Testament paradigm of wisdom. In 1 Kings 3, he asks God to give him wisdom to rule his people and immediately is faced with the dilemma of two women who both claim a baby to be their own. His resolution to their dilemma is unexpected and unpredictable, yet a demonstration of the wisdom of God. God gives us wisdom by his Spirit (1 Corinthians 2:10-16), helping us to make good choices.

AI can be used to augment or improve our decisions, but anything it outputs always needs to be interpreted by a human. We shouldn't want an AI making final decisions about medical triage or end-of-life care or deciding who gets aid first after a natural disaster. AI could make all of those decisions, yet each one of them requires wisdom and therefore needs human input. To quote Joseph Weizenbaum a second time, "Since we do not now have any ways of making computers wise, we ought not now to give computers tasks that demand wisdom."[51]

Principle 4: Justice and Mercy

The prophet Isaiah writes:

> Learn to do right; seek justice. Defend the oppressed. Take up the cause of the fatherless; plead the case of the widow. (Isaiah 1:17)

The danger with AI is that people are prone to trust the system. Despite evidence to the contrary, we tend to believe that computers get it right.

Between 1999 and 2015, there was a huge scandal in the UK Post Office. Each branch used a computer system called Horizon, but the software contained many bugs which created financial discrepancies where none existed. As a result, over 900 subpostmasters were convicted of theft, fraud, false accounting and more, despite having done nothing wrong. Some of them served jail terms, and at least one took his own life. Many others covered the shortfalls with their own money. There were warnings that the system was making mistakes, but the overwhelming approach of many of those in authority was to blindly trust the output of the computer. It ruined people's lives.

That example originates from before AI, but it's a cautionary tale for the future, as AI promises to take over more and more tasks, and make more and more decisions for us.

In the United States, an AI system was used to make risk assessments for those accused of criminal activity, with the intention that the outcome would help decide whether or not to grant bail. The issue was that the system, named COMPAS, was shown to be biased against ethnic minorities, who were therefore less likely to be granted bail. Overreliance on the "opinions" of an AI program led to injustice. AI facial recognition systems also provide more false positives with Black people, leading to more frequent wrongful arrests.

Of course, there has been plenty of injustice perpetrated without the assistance of AI throughout human history. We don't need AI's help to treat people badly! But in such cases, it's easier to spot injustice and campaign against it. When AI is behind the injustice, the decisions are opaque and harder to fight.

Alongside justice comes mercy. Micah asks:

> What does the LORD require of you? To act justly and to love mercy and to walk humbly with your God.
>
> (Micah 6:8)

When we show mercy, we're acting like our God—who does not give us what we deserve. Whether that involves a judge handing down a lesser sentence for mitigating circumstances or a bank deciding not to send in the debt-collectors following a missed payment, we instinctively recognise that there are times when mercy is appropriate.

Yet AI has no room for mercy in its calculations. It will be far more inflexible than humans in the decisions it hands down. So once again, we should be cautious about delegating decision-making as a society to AI, when it is humans whom God has called to act justly and love mercy.

What Next?

With many of the questions we've tackled so far, there are immediate actions that you can choose to take. But this chapter's topic feels more out of our control. The majority of us don't get to design and shape the systems used by large institutions across our society. We can feel powerless as we see AI being rolled out across more and more sectors.

However, we're not completely without options:

WE HAVE A CHOICE

In some areas of life, we can choose to use businesses that haven't adopted too much AI, even if it costs a little bit more. We can choose which apps we install or which online platforms we engage with. We can choose which banks we use or which insurance companies we trust. Let's vote with our feet.

WE HAVE A VOICE

As laws are passed surrounding the regulation and use of AI, we can write to our elected representatives expressing our concerns about justice, accountability or mercy. We can stand up and speak out when we see injustice happening (Proverbs 31:8-9), and speak truth in our workplaces, communities and churches.

And if you are involved in decision-making, whether that's at work or home or church, think about how you can put the principles in this chapter into practice. It's our calling to make decisions and take responsibility for them. We're to ask God for wisdom, praying that he would help us when so often the path ahead isn't clear. We're to act with justice and mercy, just as God does with us.

Discussion Questions

- How would you feel if you knew that AI had rejected you for a job without your application ever being seen by a human?
- Which types of decisions, personal or societal, do you think humans should never hand over entirely to AI? Why?
- When an AI makes a mistake, who do you instinctively think should be held responsible, and why?
- Many self-driving cars are programmed to prioritise the safety of the occupant over pedestrians in a crash. How should Christians think about using such technology in light of Jesus' call to lay down our lives for others?
- Read Isaiah 1:17. How might reliance on AI systems make it harder, or easier, to defend the oppressed?

CHAPTER 11: EVANGELISM

Can AI Help Us Share the Gospel?

We are therefore Christ's ambassadors, as though God were making his appeal through us.

2 Corinthians 5:20

Before Jesus ascended into heaven, he said to his disciples:

> All authority in heaven and on earth has been given to me. Therefore go and make disciples of all nations, baptising them in the name of the Father and of the Son and of the Holy Spirit, and teaching them to obey everything I have commanded you. And surely I am with you always, to the very end of the age.
> (Matthew 28:18-20)

This is known as the Great Commission, and it includes sharing the gospel both with our neighbours and with those in far-off lands. Is it possible that AI could be a tool to help us tell the gospel message? Are there risks we need to be aware of?

The advance of technology and the spread of the gospel have always been intertwined. The apostle Paul used ships and the Roman road network to travel across the Mediterranean and spread Christ's messages. He adopted the technology of writing on papyrus to encourage Christians to grow and mature in their faith. He has set an example for us in using technology for the sake of the kingdom.

It's an example that has been followed throughout the centuries. The early church embraced the shift from papyrus to the newly invented parchment. This allowed Scripture to spread faster and last longer, but that was nothing compared to what happened when Gutenberg invented the printing press in the 15th century. Later, long-distance shipping routes and the advent of air travel made more of the world accessible to missionaries. The radio meant that the gospel message could be broadcast into hard-to-reach regions, which accelerated with the invention of TV and then the internet. Now organisations like 100fold distribute tiny microSD cards packed full of content, including the Bible, sermons and other resources that enable people to hear the gospel in their own language.

AI for Translation

One of the greatest challenges to sharing the gospel is the language barrier. According to figures published at the end of 2025, there are 3,313 languages with no Scripture available.[52] Around 1 in 5 people are still waiting for God's word to be available in their own tongue.

A huge way that AI can help us share the gospel is therefore through translation. Perhaps this doesn't come as a surprise—generative AI is built on words and predictive text, making it well-suited for translating. I've used it on restaurant menus in Athens to work out what I'm ordering and on Chinese documents when applying for a visa.

How does this work for Bible translation? There are pitfalls—in chapter 3, on truth, we saw how AI is prone to error and full of bias, and often just makes things up. It is good at substituting words and phrases but can misunderstand metaphors and idioms. LLMs also work best with large amounts of data, which is harder in languages that have not yet been written down. But assuming that it's used with discernment, there are great opportunities here. Wycliffe Bible Translators use AI to assist humans doing the work, not to do the work for them.

In 1999, Wycliffe estimated it would take 150 years to start a Bible project in every remaining language. Now there are hopes that every person in the world might have some of the Bible available in their language by 2033. It used to take around 15 years for each language to get a full copy of the Bible. With the help of an LLM, the New Testament can now be produced in two.

In the local church, increased immigration means there is plenty of need for AI translation. Many UK churches use apps like Breeze Translate to provide live translation during services. And I regularly hear stories about people sharing the gospel across the language barrier with the use of Google Translate.

Church Chatbots?

Curious seekers are using AI to explore questions they have around faith. Many are going to ChatGPT, which tends to respond with information that mirrors their prior beliefs. Or apps are springing up like Text with Jesus,[53] which offers what it calls "meaningful conversations with spiritual advisors", by simulating Jesus, Abraham, David, Mary, Peter, John—even Adam and Eve.

This is why it could be argued that churches would benefit from AI-powered chatbots on their websites. Many people are likely to be more open with an AI than another human. They might ask the questions they're genuinely struggling with. Those too cautious to contact the church could ask the chatbot a question late at night. But there are many drawbacks, not least the ever-present problem with accuracy. Even if the model has been trained on faithful Bible content, an LLM is still just churning out text based on predictions and probability. That's not a great standard of truth and faithfulness. Imprecise or insensitive answers have the power to do great damage.

Jesus showed wisdom in knowing when to give an answer and when to reply with a question of his own—when to be clear and when to be enigmatic. He was guided by the Spirit and knew when to speak and when to remain silent. AI is never going to show that kind of discernment. It can't discern anything about the mind or heart of the person it's communicating with. With all that in mind, and also given that some people might become less proactive in evangelism if an AI chatbot purports to do it for them, the dangers of church chatbots far outweigh the benefits.

The Gospel According to Grok

A friend of mine often shares the gospel with others. One of the people he is regularly in conversation with takes his spiritual questions to GrokAI when my friend is not available, and they later discuss the answers together. That sounds like a healthy arrangement because this man has more questions than my friend has time to answer. Discussing the answers with a mature Christian reduces the risk of error.

At the same time, caution is needed. AI may give accurate answers to questions of faith and the Bible, or they may be misleading. It's often better to answer other people's questions yourself or introduce them to another Christian who might be able to help, rather than direct them to LLMs.

Other Ways to Use AI

How else could AI help you share your faith? I know Christians who use it to practise sharing the gospel—getting it to give objections that they can then respond to in real time. Others use it for brainstorming and planning outreach events, creating graphics and writing invitations. Some have used AI to help them understand their community, exploring demographic trends through data. You could use it to help people edit their spoken testimony for improved clarity and brevity.

We're only limited by our imagination, which is all the more reason for us to consider carefully what we do and don't use AI for. As we saw in chapter 7, we need to ask not just, "What do we gain?" but "What do we lose?" We need wisdom to know when AI helps us and when it gets in the way.

Mission

However well AI Bible translation can be used, it can't replace the impact of someone travelling to a far-off nation to bring people the hope of Jesus. They might spend years living in a community, working alongside the people and building relationships. There is something powerful about someone leaving the comforts of home to share the gospel with others, just as Jesus himself left the comfort of heaven to rescue us.

God's plan for reaching the nations, whether those nations are near or far, involves his people. In Acts 8, when the Ethiopian eunuch is reading the Scriptures, God brings him an evangelist to share the gospel. In Acts 9, Paul meets with the risen Jesus on the road to Damascus but is then sent to meet with Ananias for further instructions. In Acts 10, when Cornelius prays, the angelic vision is insufficient—Peter is required to share the good news with him and his household.

In each case, God's method was not the most efficient use of resources. It often isn't. It may seem weak and slow, but God's plan for reaching the nations is through ordinary believers sharing the gospel, often falteringly. AI isn't going to change that. If we use translation for church services, it needs to go alongside English classes or raising up people who know the language in question. Only a more personal approach will facilitate the kind of long-term connections and deep relationships that can change people's hearts and lives.

AI can help us share the gospel. But it can't share the gospel for us. That's a job God has given to the church. We are his ambassadors, declaring the message of Christ (2 Corinthians 5:20).

Telling the Gospel Story in the Age of AI

I could be proved wrong, but I expect AI to bring a cultural shift on a par with the invention of the printing press or the Industrial Revolution. It will bring disruption to our lives and questions about our place in the world. Musician Nick Cave recently said, "People need meaning and the secular world didn't come up with the goods".[54] I think the AI revolution will reveal the shallow foundations of so many people's worldviews.

Christians need to be ready to tell a better story about God—about the world, about us and about AI. The questions we've covered chapter by chapter aren't only being asked by Christians—you only need to look at the news to see that everyone's wondering what makes humans different from AI.

Everyone's worried about what is true or what to do when AI takes their job. As we saw in chapter 6, the current isolation problem is epidemic. Christians have an opportunity to tell people God's good news in this confusing world. This, for me, is more exciting than whether AI can share the gospel for us.

AI and Death

Something I've always found fascinating is how those on the forefront of the AI development have dreams of transhumanism (uploading their minds to the cloud so they can live for ever). Unlike many of the things I've described, I don't think it will ever happen, but the fact that people want it, envision it, write stories about it and invest billions of dollars to develop it is telling.

Others want to use AI to fight the consequences of death: grief and pain. One website called Seance AI, offers the chance to upload a record of all your conversations with a deceased loved one and then promises to adopt their personality for ongoing connection. Their website claims:

> Here is where AI meets the afterlife, love endures beyond the veil. Start your adventure today and let your loved ones speak to your heart once again.[55]

In late 2025, an advert for 2Wai went viral.[56] In it, a digital avatar of a woman chats to her pregnant daughter, offering life advice, and later does the same for her grandson. The idea is that she created the avatar through this company before she died and that, for her relatives, communicating this way is as good as talking to the real person.

All this ties into something that we recognise as humans: the pain of separation and death—the wrongness of it all. Yet it seeks to solve the problem in a way that is infinitely inferior to what God offers. It's no more than the creation of an echo or a ghost. Again, Christians can tell the better story about how Jesus has truly defeated death and his followers will rise in glory to be with him for ever.

Conversations about meaning, truth and even the end of the world are increasing, partly because AI brings these questions to the fore. The apostle Peter tells us, "Always be prepared to give an answer to everyone who asks you to give the reason for the hope that you have" (1 Peter 3:15). Yes, let's utilise AI to share the gospel, but, more foundationally, let's be ready to share the gospel in the tumultuous age of AI.

Discussion Questions

- How have you shared the gospel with others in ways that wouldn't have been technologically possible a century ago?
- Read Acts 2:5–11. What does this passage suggest about God's concern that people hear the gospel in their own language? Can we use AI to help us bridge the language gap?
- Are you excited about the prospect of using AI to help you share the gospel? In what practical ways do you think it could help you?
- What do we learn from the fact that God uses (weak and inefficient) humans to tell others about Jesus? What would be lost if evangelism became more efficient but less relational?
- Read 1 Peter 3:15. Have you had any conversations with friends or family members about AI? What fears or concerns did they express? How would you answer them with biblical hope?

CHAPTER 12: FUTURE

Do I Need to Fear What's Ahead?

He is before all things,
and in him all things hold together.

Colossians 1:17

In an interview with the BBC in 2014, Stephen Hawking said:

> I think the development of full artificial intelligence could spell the end of the human race. Once humans develop artificial intelligence, it will take off on its own and redesign itself at an ever-increasing rate. Humans, who are limited by slow biological evolution, couldn't compete, and would be superseded.[57]

Do you share his fear? Many who work in the AI industry do. In a 2023 survey of AI engineers,[58] around half of them estimated a greater than 10% chance of human extinction (or severe disempowerment) through our inability to control AI. Again in 2023, an open letter called for an immediate pause in AI development. What was remarkable was that it was signed by many of the people involved in AI, including the CEO of X and the co-founder of Apple. It read:

> AI systems with human-competitive intelligence can pose profound risks to society and humanity.[59]

Perhaps this is precisely what you worry about. Each time you read the news, you become a little bit more fearful of what the future holds. Or maybe you think that the warnings are all hype; when these entrepreneurs highlight the existential dangers of AI, it's just part of their marketing strategy.

The Tale of Peril

In chapter 1, we thought about *the tale of promise*—the idea that AI will solve our problems and lead us to new heights as a species. But there's also a *tale of peril*. It tells us that ushering in AI is opening Pandora's box, inviting chaos and destruction, which will not end well. Generally, there are three categories of risk that people highlight.

RISK 1: MISUSE BY PEOPLE

First is the potential for AI to be misused by sinful people, or what the world calls "bad actors". Terrorists using AI to hack critical infrastructure or design chemical weapons; governments using AI for warfare or to systematically oppress certain people groups; companies using AI to maximise profits and exploit consumers; or individuals using "nudification" apps to create naked images of real people.

In addition, we're already seeing AI used to undermine democracy. In January 2024, automated telephone messages with the voice of Joe Biden were sent to New Hampshire voters, telling Democrats not to vote in the primary and to "save their vote for the November election". In Slovakia in 2023, two days before an election, a fake audio recording emerged of a party leader apparently talking to a journalist about rigging the election. It was later debunked as false, but it will have swayed some voters.

RISK 2: UNINTENDED CONSEQUENCES

Facebook was first released while I was still at university. Access was really limited, and my friends and I thought it was a bit silly. We laughed at this new face-book thing. Imagine if someone had explained at the time how it would shape the world over the next 20 years. As a result of Facebook and other social media, we have chronic addiction, information overload, shortened attention spans, mental health challenges, resurgence in conspiracy theories, increased loneliness, fake news and more.

If you had told me all that would happen, I wouldn't have believed you. This is the reality of unintended consequences: often, you can't even predict what they'll be. But every technology has them. The tale of peril reminds us that when it comes to AI, we don't yet know what the negative outcomes will be for our world.

RISK 3: CIVILISATIONAL COLLAPSE

In terms of severity, this risk is top of the pile, with the kinds of consequences that could involve the destruction of humanity. This is the fear that drives sci-fi plots.

In The Terminator franchise, Skynet, a military AI system, reaches the level of self-awareness. It immediately perceives humanity as a threat, so it launches a global nuclear attack, leading to a great war between humanity and machines.

In The Matrix franchise, humans have been enslaved by

sentient machines and are just used as batteries to provide electricity for the robots' needs.

In *Avengers: Age of Ultron*, Ultron becomes sentient and concludes that the only way to bring peace to the world is to eradicate humanity.

Those are all stories of creation usurping the creator, which makes them fascinating echoes of the Bible's narrative: that we, the created, have rebelled against our Creator. Some think these threats are existential and we should pull the plug on AI immediately. Others think it's all overblown. Your response probably has as much to do with your personality and disposition as anything else.

Three Steady Anchors

When we face an uncertain outlook, Jesus is who we look to. Here are three ways he helps us to navigate the future, whatever AI might bring.

1. RULE OF CHRIST

There's a scene in the old Disney animation *Fantasia* that's set to the music of "The Sorcerer's Apprentice". In it, the old sorcerer leaves the room with instructions for his young apprentice to tidy up. Looking for a shortcut, he casts a spell to animate a broom, but things quickly spiral out of control, as enchanted brooms carrying water flood the workshop. Every attempt to stop them only makes the deluge worse. This is the story of a rogue intelligence (albeit powered by magic rather than microchips) that has escaped human control. In the end, the sorcerer returns and restores order to the chaos.

The apprentice created something beyond his control, but he was unable to create something beyond his master's. In a similar way, we may create an AI that we cannot control, but nothing escapes God's rule. Dutch theologian Abraham Kuyper famously said:

> There is not a square inch in the whole domain of our human existence over which Christ, who is Sovereign over all, does not cry: "Mine!"[60]

It's reassuring to be reminded of God's sovereignty over all of human history and even, though it's hard for us to understand, over sin and evil. (See Isaiah 45:7 or Daniel 4:35.) We could update Kuyper's quote to say that there is not one algorithm, not one AI, not one word uttered by ChatGPT over which Christ does not cry, "Mine!" He is sovereign over it all.

Paul tells us in Colossians 1:16-17:

> For in him all things were created: things in heaven and on earth, visible and invisible, whether thrones or powers or rulers or authorities; all things have been created through him and for him. He is before all things, and in him all things hold together. (Colossians 1:16-17)

We do not need to fear. In fact, our situation is far more favourable than in the Disney animation. Unlike the sorcerer, who is absent, by upholding all things at all times, Christ never leaves the room.

2. REST IN CHRIST

The fact that Christ is now ruling and reigning doesn't mean that things will be easy. We're still waiting for the full arrival of his kingdom, when death and mourning will be no more (Revelation 21:4), and sorrow and sighing will flee away (Isaiah 35:10). As we've seen, there are many ways that our lives could be upended by the AI revolution. So what do we do when everything seems to go wrong? We rest in Christ.

Psalm 46 describes a situation where the earth gives way and the mountains are moved into the heart of the sea (v 2). Everything seems to be crumbling, yet that psalm begins and ends by reassuring us with these truths:

> God is our refuge and strength, an ever-present help in trouble. (v 1)

> The Lord Almighty is with us; the God of Jacob is our fortress. (v 11)

Jesus never leaves us or forsakes us. We're invited in Philippians 4 not to "be anxious about anything, but in every situation, by prayer and petition, with thanksgiving, present your requests to God. And the peace of God, which transcends all understanding, will guard your hearts and your minds in Christ Jesus." (v 6-7). This means that while we may have concern about the future, we do not need to be anxious about it. You can pray about your fears, telling God what worries you, and receive his peace. Jesus, our Good Shepherd, poured out his life for us on the cross. He has been carrying us through life, and nothing about the AI revolution will cause him to put us down.

3. RETURN OF CHRIST

As Christians, we can be confident that Stephen Hawking's fears will not become reality—humanity will not be replaced.

When he came into this world, God the Son—the second person of the Trinity—united himself to humanity. He took on our flesh, becoming like us in every way (yet without sin). This was not a temporary assignment. Even now, in glory, Christ is fully God and fully man. We know that AI will not usurp humanity because in order to do so, it would have to usurp him. He is the head of humanity, our great representative and champion. Our future is as secure as the foundation of Christ's throne.

In Daniel 7, there is a vision of the "Son of Man". The curtain is pulled back for Daniel to see God the Son being given all authority by God the Father. Daniel says:

> He was given authority, glory and sovereign power; all nations and peoples of every language worshipped him. His dominion is an everlasting dominion that will not pass away, and his kingdom is one that will never be destroyed. (v 14)

Christ's kingdom cannot be destroyed. We know that God has a plan for history. We don't know every point on the journey, but we do know the destination, because God has...

> ... made known to us the mystery of his will according to his good pleasure, which he purposed in Christ, to be put into effect when the times reach their fulfilment—*to bring unity to all things in heaven and on earth under Christ.* (Ephesians 1:9-10)

History will conclude with Christ returning in glory and reigning over all. On that day, your fears about AI will vanish like the morning mist. Any suffering you have experienced as a result of the AI revolution will not only be shown to be light and momentary in comparison with what God will give you then, but you will see how God has used that suffering for his good purposes.

> What, then, shall we say in response to these things? If God is for us, who can be against us? He who did not spare his own Son, but gave him up for us all—

> how will he not also, along with him, graciously give us all things? (Romans 8:31-32)

Nothing can separate you from the love of Christ! Instead of fearing the future with AI, because of these three truths, Christians can respond with faith. We don't need to know what the future holds if we know who holds the future. We don't need to fear what is coming when Jesus casts out all fear.

How Should We Use AI?

In this book, I've encouraged you to use AI wisely, thoughtfully and cautiously, yet thankfully. Here are my final suggestions to take hold of as we move into the age of AI.

- Remember that AI only ever has "apparent" intelligence.
- Remember that AI is often inaccurate, and that we will need increased discernment and wisdom in the years ahead.
- Don't use AI in a way that isolates you and disconnects you from other people.
- Don't use AI as a replacement for deep thought and learning.
- Use AI in ways that honour the dignity of other humans and don't undermine them.
- Use AI in ways that honour God and bring glory to his name.

> So whether you eat or drink or whatever you do, do it all for the glory of God. (1 Corinthians 10:31)

Discussion Questions

- Are you optimistic or pessimistic about the future with AI? Which of the dangers of AI do you worry about the most?
- Do you believe that God is sovereign over all AI? Does this help you not to fear that AI might spiral out of control?
- Read Romans 8:31–39. Which of Paul's assurances feels most relevant to fears about AI, and why?
- What specific things can Christians pray for as AI continues to develop?
- After reading this book, what's one way in which you might stop using AI? What's one way in which you might start using it?

Acknowledgements

There are many people to thank for making this book possible. To Sophie, Phoebe and Sol, thank you for putting up with the many extra hours I've had to work, and for your encouragement and enthusiasm.

To everyone at CARE. James, thank you firstly for tasking me with becoming our resident expert on AI, and then for supporting this project; and thank you to Ian and Stuart for your encouragement as brothers-in-arms.

Thank you to Mothew and Toni, for giving me advice and input at an early stage of this project, and to Reuben T, for author-to-author encouragement.

Thank you to everyone who has chatted with me about AI, discussed and debated it, or sent me articles. That list is too long to be included here, but particular thanks to those who gave up time for longer interviews: Dave B, Rich O, Jonathan G, Mark W-T and John H.

Thank you to Catherine and everyone at The Good Book Company for taking me on as a first-time author.

And most of all, my thanks are to God, the Great Creator. My prayer is that you will use this book to build your people and bring glory to your name.

ENDNOTES

1 David Betts, *The Church and AI: Seven Guidelines for Ministry on the Digital Frontiers* (Ingram Content Group UK Limited, Milton Keynes UK, 2024), p. 33.

2 www.darioamodei.com/post/the-urgency-of-interpretability (accessed on 12 January 2026).

3 www.youtube.com/watch?v=xoVJKj8lcNQ (accessed on 12 January 2026).

4 www.theguardian.com/technology/2025/aug/04/demis-hassabis-ai-future-10-times-bigger-than-industrial-revolution-and-10-times-faster (accessed on 18 January 2026).

5 https://doi.bio/demis_hassabi (accessed on 24 January 2026).

6 www.youtube.com/watch?v=_5XvDCjrdXs&t=63s (accessed on 12 January 2026).

7 Same as previous endnote.

8 https://youtu.be/B3IeRplsYXw?si=7iytN8MzpV2C_JwO&t=3485 (accessed on 12 January 2026).

9 Poll conducted by Searchlight Institute in August 2025. Surveyed 2,301 American adults. Question 91. www.searchlightinstitute.org/wp-content/uploads/2025/12/Searchlight-AI-Survey-Toplines.pdf (accessed on 12 January 2026).

10 www.thegospelcoalition.org/ai-christian-benchmark/ (accessed on 13 January 2026).

11 www.bbc.co.uk/news/uk-67302048 (accessed on 13 January 2026).

12 www.axios.com/2025/05/28/ai-jobs-white-collar-unemployment-anthropic (accessed on 14 January 2026).

13 Channel 4, "Will AI Take My Job?" (documentary, broadcast 20 October 2025), citing a Survation poll of 1,000 adults.

14 www.fortune.com/2025/07/05/ford-ceo-jim-farley-ai-white-collar-jobs-essential-economy-skilled-trade-jobs-shortage/ (accessed on 14 January 2026).

15 Tim Keller, *Every Good Endeavour* (Hodder & Stoughton, 2012), p. 37.

16 www.youtube.com/watch?v=kND0iGErBk8&t=227s (accessed on 14 January 2026).

17 www.christianitytoday.com/2025/11/solomon-ray-ai-christian-music-soul-singer/ (accessed on 15 January 2026)

18 Same as previous endnote.

19 Alastair Gordon, *Why Art Matters: A Call for Christians to Create* (InterVarsity Press, 2021), p. 3.

20 Philip Hefner, *The Human Factor: Evolution, Culture and Religion* (Fortress Press, Minneapolis, 1993).

21 www.theguardian.com/technology/2025/jun/03/creatives-academics-rejecting-ai-at-home-work (accessed on 16 January 2026).

22 www.youtube.com/watch?v=3lPnN8omdPA&t=178s (accessed on 16 January 2026).

23 Makoto Fujimura, *Art + Faith: A Theology of Making* (Yale University Press, 2019), p. xiii.

24 www.merriam webster.com/wordplay/word-of-the-year (accessed on 16 January 2026).

25 www.breitbart.com/tech/2025/05/26/former-meta-exec-nick-clegg-artists-demands-over-ai-copyright-laws-implausible-would-kill-the-industry (accessed on 15 January 2026).

26 www.theguardian.com/technology/2025/oct/22/im-suddenly-so-angry-my-strange-unnerving-week-with-an-ai-friend (accessed on 15 January 2026).

27 www.cambridge.org/news-and-insights/parasocial-is-cambridge-dictionary-word-of-the-year-2025 (accessed on 15 January 2026).

28 www.dwarkesh.com/p/mark-zuckerberg-2?timestamp=1734.0 (accessed on 15 January 2026).

29 onlinelibrary.wiley.com/doi/10.1002/mar.21899 (accessed on 15 January 2026).

30 www.telegraph.co.uk/us/news/2025/06/19/married-father-ai-chatbot-girlfriend (accessed on 15 January 2026).

31 www.theatlantic.com/magazine/2025/12/ai-companionship-anti-social-media/684596 (accessed on 15 January 2026).

32 C. S. Lewis, *The Four Loves* (HarperCollins, 1960), p. 74.

33 www.theguardian.com/us news/2025/aug/29/chatgpt-suicide-openai-sam-altman-adam-raine (accessed on 15 January 2026). Note: This article contains distressing content.

34 Tim Keller, *The Meaning of Marriage* (Hodder & Stoughton, 2011), p. 95.

35 www.pmccentral.nih.gov/articles/PMC11871827 (accessed on 15 January 2026).

36 www.telegraph.co.uk/news/2025/12/25/chatbots-mental-health-warning-nhs-chief (accessed on 15 January 2026).

37 Savanta, Student Generative AI Survey 2025, poll of 1,041 full-time undergraduates; www.smartthinking.org.uk/report/student-generative-ai-survey-2025 (accessed on 16 January 2026).

38 www.christianitytoday.com/2025/05/gloo-ai-artificial-intelligence-church-worship-tech-ethics (accessed on 29 October 2025).

39 Often wrongly attributed to Marshall McLuhan. "A Schoolman's Guide to Marshall McLuhan" by John M. Culkin SJ (Saturday Review, 18 March 1967); https://webspace.royalroads.ca/llefevre/wp-content/uploads/sites/258/2017/08/A-Schoolmans-Guide-to-Marshall-McLuhan-1.pdf.

40 www.techradar.com/computing/artificial-intelligence/are-you-polite-to-chatgpt-heres-where-you-rank-among-ai-chatbot-users (accessed on 16 January 2026). Research conducted in 2024 by Future.

41 Same as previous endnote.

42 www.anthropic.com/research/end-subset-conversations (accessed on 16 January 2026).

43 www.x.com/sama/status/1912646035979239430 (accessed on 16 January 2026).

44 www.livescience.com/technology/artificial-intelligence/being-mean-to-chatgpt-increases-its-accuracy-but-you-may-end-up-regretting-it-scientists-warn (accessed on 16 January 2026).

45 Todd Korpi, *AI Goes to Church: Pastoral Wisdom for Artificial Intelligence* (InterVarsity Press, 2025), p. 62.

46 www.edubirdie.com/blog/gen-z-and-ai-consciousness-careers-and-chatbot-confessions (accessed on 16 January 2026).

47 www.washingtonpost.com/technology/2022/06/11/google-ai-lamda-blake-lemoine (accessed on 16 January 2026).

48 www.premierchristian.news/en/news/article/hundreds-attend-german-church-service-led-by-avatars (accessed on 17 January 2026).

49 www.youtube.com/watch?v=CIMZH7DEPPQ (accessed on 17 January 2026).

50 Joseph Weizenbaum, *Computer Power and Human Reason: From Judgment to Calculation* (W. H. Freeman, 1976), p. 227.

51 Same as previous endnote.

52 https://wycliffe.org.uk/statistics (accessed on 19 January 2026).

53 www.textwith.me/en/jesus (accessed on 17 January 2026).

54 www.thetimes.com/culture/music/article/nick-cave-interview-bad-seeds-wild-god-album-7qgl8p8kj (accessed on 19 January 2026).

55 www.ae.studio/seanceai (accessed on 17 January 2026).

56 www.youtube.com/watch?v=UFenaK4wIsw (accessed on 17 January 2026).

57 www.bbc.co.uk/news/technology-30290540 (accessed on 18 January 2026).

58 aiimpacts.org/wp-content/uploads/2023/04/Thousands_of_AI_authors_on_the_future_of_AI.pdf, p. 14 (accessed on 18 January 2026).

59 www.futureoflife.org/open-letter/pause-giant-ai-experiments (accessed on 18 January 2026).

60 Abraham Kuyper, *A Centennial Reader* (The Patternoster Press, 1998), p. 488

thegoodbook COMPANY

BIBLICAL | RELEVANT | ACCESSIBLE

At The Good Book Company we are dedicated to helping Christians and local churches grow. We believe that God's growth process always starts with hearing clearly what he has said to us through his timeless and flawless word—the Bible.

Ever since we opened our doors in 1991, we have been striving to produce resources that are biblical, relevant, and accessible. By God's grace, we have grown to become an international publisher, encouraging ordinary Christians of every age and stage and every background and denomination to live for Christ day by day and equipping churches to grow in their knowledge of God, their love for one another, and the effectiveness of their outreach.

Call one of our friendly team for a discussion of your needs or visit one of our local websites for more information on the resources and services we provide.

Your friends at The Good Book Company

thegoodbook.com | thegoodbook.co.uk
thegoodbook.com.au | thegoodbook.co.nz